INTRODUCTION

A true inspiring story of a woman who went through a harrowing life and found courage, hope, love and faith.

"I wrote this book to help others who may be going through life experiences that are not pleasant.

I was once ashamed of my life and kept blaming myself as not being worthy.

I realised that it was a lie of the enemy.

God does love me, I did it and I pray that you will overcome too."

Some of the names in this book have been changed to protect their identity.

CHAPTERS

Childhood

I am an Indian girl born in 1966 and lived in a terraced house with Mum and Dad, three brothers and one sister. I'm the youngest in the family and growing up I remember Mum being poorly. The house we lived in had two bedrooms, two living rooms, kitchen and a downstairs bathroom. The two older brothers shared one bedroom and the rest of us shared the other room. I remember the eldest brother getting married, so the brother he shared the bedroom with had to move onto the bed settee downstairs. I only knew brother was sleeping downstairs because I kept going to the bathroom and disturbing his sleep.

My Mum was not well, I remember her lying down on the settee a lot; she would do the cooking and cleaning and then lay down again. The front room was kept tidy and it was used for guests only; we only used the living room. Going in and out of the house was always by the back door. As it was a terraced house, the garden was in two sections and an alley after about four houses to get onto the main street.

In the garden was a single swing. One afternoon my sister was on the swing and happened to fall off and hurt herself, I wasn't happy because my dad took the swing down; now there was nothing to play with.

I am growing up now, I'm going to the nursery and I remember Mum taking me to the school and I was crying "don't leave me here," the teachers took hold of me and told my Mum to go. It's ok now as it is break time and we get to have a carton of milk with a biscuit.

I remember the school having a medical day when a doctor and nurse came to check our well-being. The nurse asked me to remove my clothing which I did but keeping my vest and underwear on. My weight was checked and my height was checked, I was holding on to my pants and the nurse was asking me if I was OK and if I had been touched by someone down below. I replied No! This was a lie, as I did not want to get into trouble. After my check-up I was given a bottle of vitamin medicine to take home.

I remember trying to fasten the zip on my coat holding the bottle of medicine between my legs, when the bottle then slipped and fell to the floor; I picked it up and carried on home. I did not realise that the bottle had cracked and I was all sticky. My school was on the next road from my house and I walked home by myself.

I would go to the shop on my own which was at the top of our street to buy sweets. Once I was walking towards the shop when I saw a man looking at me and showing me a bag of sweets, I stopped and looked at him, then looked down at his ankle and I saw a knife showing from his sock; he also looked down at his ankle. I ran home not telling anyone what had happened.

I remember mum being in hospital and the older brother had dinner ready. After dinner we went to visit mum in hospital, there was a lady sitting in the chair next to her and says to me that I can have a balloon, I looked at her and didn't move until I saw my mum say it was ok to get one.

I am about seven years old and feeling so scared within; I felt alone. We did not have hugs from our parents and it felt strict but at the same time we were provided for as we had food and clothes to wear; but we did not have any toys to play with.

I have come home with a doll and Mum asked me "where did you get it from?" I looked at her and I said that the lady across the road had given it to me. Mum says nothing and I go and play with my doll, she has blonde hair and came with clothes. The truth was that I stole the doll from the shop and I had lied to my Mum. I don't know why I lied, but I get sick to my stomach from keeping secrets.

I was abused by someone the family knew; I was given two pennies and told to keep quiet about it. Which I did and I felt different than the others.

Dad was working full-time and we were moving from a two bedroom house to a three bedroom house. The house is massive and it has three bedrooms and an upstairs bathroom, three rooms downstairs with a kitchen, larder room and an outside toilet.

I will be starting junior school soon. Going to school each morning my stomach would churn and I would constantly need the toilet. I would avoid drinking tea before school thinking that would be better. Our classroom was a mobile class and at break-time we could buy snacks to eat. I wanted to buy crisps that cost three pence; I had ten pence to spend for the week so I used that. The teacher said to me that she has no change and that I will have to wait to get it.

Now it's time to go home and the teacher still has not given me my change. I tell my brother Ricky about it as he goes to the same school and he said to go and tell the teacher. But I couldn't, something inside me froze, I was scared, I feared I was going to get into trouble. I never did ask for my change and the teacher never remembered.

Another day at school and I'm talking with my friend Jade, she's got fifty pence and she puts it in her desk drawer. I went into her drawer and took it. At the end of the school day she notices her money is gone and tells the teacher. Everyone has been asked and I kept quiet. Although the teacher asked me about it saying I knew it was there; I still kept quiet.

I had the money, going school the next day I called for a friend on the way. As I waited for my friend in the hallway of her home, I put the fifty pence in her pocket. When she put her coat on and put her hand in her pocket, she found the money and took it out.

She was so happy that she said "Oh my Mum put it in my pocket". On the way to school we stopped at the sweet shop and she spent the money that I put in her pocket.

At school, I have been called to the head masters office and I know why, I'm in trouble for stealing the money. The headmaster takes me over his knee and gives me three lashes with the slipper.

At home I have written an apology letter which I take to school and give to the head teacher. I have now been questioned about the letter. He asked why it was in my writing. I told him that my mum cannot write English so I had to write it and she signed it. That was not true because I had signed it. Every week I would have 10p pocket money and I saved it and gave it back to Jade.

At home there wasn't much to do as we didn't have many games to play with, but I remember that there were tokens on HP sauce bottles to collect, so every time the shopping was done and we bought HP sauce I would cut out the token and send them off and receive a jigsaw puzzle. I've collected four in total and when I had completed a jigsaw I would glue it down on some card and it became a picture.

Mum didn't like us playing outside the house, so when I knew some friends were playing outside I would go into the garden and crawl underneath the dining room window so I could sneak out of the back door. Mum would always knock on the window and call me back in and I would think "how did she know." Why couldn't I play outside when other kids are? I'd ask; she'd tell me that girls don't play in the streets.

I would draw on the ground with chalk a hopscotch game and play. The eldest brother Paul was strict and he made rules that I couldn't play with marbles or with playing cards; I could never understand why? Now that he is married with children they have bought their own house and have moved out.

I was crying because I didn't understand why they were leaving. He would say "it's ok I am still going to be coming round to visit."

On one occasion my other brother Ricky and I decided to play cards in the bedroom and we locked the door. We had been playing for hours when all of a sudden there was a knock on the bedroom door, nobody spoke, then Ricky opened the door and there stood Paul, he said that there was a phone call for Ricky, so Ricky made his way downstairs. I was going to follow when Paul grabbed my hair and said "where do you think you're going?" then I said "I'm going to tell mum" and he slapped my face saying "who said you can play cards?"

Ricky and I would get up to all sorts of things. He was two years older than me and we would make up our own games. One time, when we were in the bedroom, which had two beds, one opposite each other; we were jumping on them. We were having a great time and laughing a lot, until we get hold of some talcum powder and started shaking it. All of a sudden our laughter stopped, the lid came off and the powder is all over the beds. Oh no! Footsteps are coming up the stairs and Mum is asking what we are both up to? We started to turn the quilts the other way around; which we did. Then, when Mum came into the room, she saw it looking like dust. All of a sudden she turned the quilts back and her face turned to horror as she saw the full mess we had made. She scolded us, got hold of me and smacked me. Ricky ran out of the room laughing at me. I am crying and telling Mum that I'm going to wet myself and I need the toilet; so I run.

At the weekend Ricky and I go to the local swimming baths, and as I'm not a very good swimmer, I have a rubber ring to wear. I'm standing by the side of the pool with the ring around my waist, when I jumped into the water I didn't know that the ring would stay on the water and I went through it.

I couldn't swim, I'm struggling and eventually Ricky decides to pull me up; after that I didn't like swimming.

In school, however, we had to have swimming classes and I forgot all about my previous experience as I enjoyed playing in the swimming baths. Again, I had a rubber ring around my waist and decided to jump in the water. I jumped into the water with the ring on and the ring went and caught my feet; holding me upside down in the water. I'm struggling to get out and trying to get someone's attention when the teacher saw me and asked another girl to help me out. I kept taking swimming lessons and finally learnt how to swim. I achieved a red badge for swimming a length of the pool.

I am starting secondary school now and I was hoping to go to the same school as Ricky and my sister Manpreet. I'm the youngest of the five, Ricky is two years older than me and Manpreet is four years older than me and they got to travel by bus, I thought I would be going to the same school.

Mum has said that I had to go to the school near home; it was a twenty minute walk away. I wanted to go to the same school and didn't understand why I was being treated differently. I found out though, that my friends were going to the same school I was going to.

Manpreet and Ricky would stay for school dinners and I would have to come home. In winter it would get difficult to walk the journey home; then I would have school meals. At the weekends I would wash my shirt; I would wash the collars and the cuffs as we didn't have a washing machine.

There were times when I forgot to wash my shirt and wore it dirty. Friends would say to me that my shirt is dirty at the collar and I would say that my Mum forgot to wash it. I remember Mum not being well and she'd always be lying down on the settee in the mornings.

One morning as I was getting ready for school my hair needed combing, I asked Mum to do it. She said to ask Manpreet as she is not feeling well. Manpreet would part my hair and then I would do plaits. I didn't eat breakfast before going to school as it would upset my stomach. Many times Mum would say I don't eat and I should have breakfast, so I told her my stomach gets upset.

It's going to be games at school today, I'm not keen on P.E. and as it's raining it's going to be indoors. Today it's on the trampoline. I hadn't been on the trampoline before and its fun jumping up and bouncing until I started to feel sick; later in the day I'm physically sick. After a few days off school I go to the doctors, no one goes with me and that made me uncomfortable. I had a sense of loneliness as I went on my own. The doctor checked me and gave me some medicine.

The weather is nice now and it's the weekend, Manpreet and I went to the park with some friends. While we were there, we saw some other friends we knew who were in a boat that they had rowed to the end of the lake. They asked my friends and me to come into the boat and they would get out. I'm standing on the side of the lake holding onto the boat and my friend jumps in. While I'm still holding onto the boat it starts to drift out into the lake. I should have let go of the boat but I didn't and I was being stretched out; lost my balance and fell into the water.

The bottom of the lake was so disgusting! I did not think I'd be able to get out again. Eventually I did manage to get to the side of the water again and climb out of the lake. This was the worst thing that could happen because I didn't like wearing wet clothes. While all the others were laughing Manpreet was saying "wait until you get home you're going to be in so much trouble," as if I cared. Manpreet grassed me up to Mum, but Mum never said much so I went and got cleaned up.

It is going to be school holidays soon and each class has a school play to perform. In our class the topic was about sharing and they needed one pupil to play the one that would be left out, I put my hand up and said I would like that part. I wanted to do that part because I thought I would be in the background. The other parts included being parents and students with an attitude. The day of our play is here and I'm nervous, I was wrong when I chose the part to play; I was not in the background but the main character right in the front. The play was applauded by the headmaster and he said to me that I played the part so well that it looked real. My emotions were real in the play, they didn't know. I played the victim of being bullied and singled out by the class and parents.

I enjoy working with my Dad he does all his own DIY, as well as working three shifts in his normal job. He is building his own wooden shed at the back of the garden and I was always eager to help, I would pass him the tools and be so happy because it would make me feel wanted. The shed was the size of a garage. When he had finished building it, I asked if I could help to paint it. I liked to paint and in the past I had asked if I could paint the stair railings. However, the job was given to Manpreet even though I had asked first. I even enjoyed helping put the paste on the wallpaper and I would watch dad put the paper on the wall and how he would line up the patterns.

In the evening Dad got ready to go to the pub, Ricky, Manpreet, Mum and I would be watching television. I would get a nudge and Ricky or Manpreet would whisper to me to ask dad if he could buy us some chocolates. Dad would look at me and smile, but Mum would always give me a look as if to say no. I would always be told to ask and I'm the one who always got told off for asking. Mum would say that I got pocket money and wasn't that enough.

No, it wasn't enough and wasn't right because I got twenty five pence a week while Ricky and Manpreet got fifty pence each. Mum said it's because they are older than me. How did that work out? We all ate sweets and it still wasn't enough.

On school days I would come home for lunch and then go back for the afternoon. After lunch I would walk past the pub where my Dad was, I knew he would be sitting in the window seat, always in the same place. I would see him with a mate playing cards and I would go and tap on the window. Whilst standing on my toes I wave to my dad and a big smile appears on my face. Dad would get some change out of his pocket and drop it through the open window. I never told anyone about this and I kept it between Dad and me.

When it came to the weekly shopping, which was done at the weekend, I would have to go with my mum because Manpreet always refused to go. I couldn't understand what her problem was; I'd tell her that you only have to pull the trolley. It was the trolley that carried the shopping, this had two wheels and because no one liked pulling it, I had to. I didn't really mind but I would walk fast and leave Mum behind. I can hear her shouting telling me to slow down and that I was just like my Dad, always walking fast and ahead; that put a big smile on my face.

I remember this and still laugh at it today. Mum once asked me to buy a loaf of bread from the local store and gave me fifty pence. On the walk down the road I was wondering if a fifty pence coin can roll. I give it a go and it rolled and rolled and dropped down a drain. Oh no! What have I done? I'm going to be in trouble! I went to the shop and got a loaf of bread anyway telling the shop keeper that my Mum will pay for the bread later. When I got home Mum asked me for the change and I said I had spent it on sweets; she never questioned it and I was scared to tell the truth.

Another time, when I'm in the bathroom, I see my Dad's shaving kit. As I'm looking to see how the blade fits the safety razor I pretend to shave.

I try it on my eyebrows and Oops! I've slit my eyebrow. Oh no! What have I done? I am panicking and I put his gear away, I tried to mess the eyebrow up so it wouldn't be noticeable. The next day when I woke up I was hoping it had all gone away, but when I looked in the mirror it was still there. I even put spit on my eyebrow to create a tangled look. Mum has called me to help wring out the washing in the garden and she's looking sternly at my face. What have you done to your eyebrow? I cut it with Dad's shaving razor because it slipped in my hand. I was scared I was going to get in trouble, but she never told me off.

During the holidays I would go and stay at my cousin's house for a few days, I enjoyed those times as we would go around town and get to enjoy takeaway food. When I'd get home Mum would say that I've changed when I stay away from home and that I wouldn't be allowed to do it again. I promised I would not change and not to stop my visits.

Now my sister-in-law Ruby has come over to our house to visit. I like Ruby. While I'm in the kitchen washing the dishes she comes and talks to me. Whilst we are talking, I come out with telling her that I've got a secret that no one knows about. I told her that when I was young I was touched; she asked me if I had told Mum. I told her that I cannot tell anyone or I will be in trouble, but she said I wouldn't be in any trouble.

I enjoy cooking and I've cut some potatoes to make chips and having them with beans, when Ricky comes in and says he'll have some too. So I give him the portion I've just made and I start peeling potatoes again cutting them thinly to fry. A cousin turns up and wants some chips as well and I also serve him. When I looked for more potatoes to peel there was none left.

I went without and they said they were tasty. I asked Mum if there were any more potatoes, she replied "you should have eaten them when you cooked it."

I was always trying to please others. I would live with an unsettled feeling and it wouldn't go away.

I've cooked my Dad some chapattis and curry and while I'm in the kitchen I heard him raise his voice at me. He was saying that it's better to make crooked chapattis than having them uncooked as it can upset the stomach. I was so upset and scared to come out of the kitchen; Mum said it was OK.

Today is my birthday and I'm sixteen. I have come home from school and I see that my Dad was home from work and lying on the sofa. He is not well and a doctor has been called. The doctor said that he was suffering from a temperature and his blood pressure was high. In the evening sister-in-law Ruby came round with a birthday cake for me, it was the first birthday cake I have ever had and it was in a model of a Princess wearing a blue gown. I am telling everyone to look at the cake but Mum said "Your Dad is sick and all you can think about is the cake; a sad look is on my face. He was sick on my previous birthday and again now; after a few days dad is well and goes back to work.

Mum and Dad have been planning a trip to India and I'm also excited because we will be having the house to ourselves which has never happened before. But Mum has said that I will have to go with them as they are not going to leave me at home with my brother and sister even though I'm sixteen years old. I couldn't understand why; but I was excited to be going away on a trip.

We went for six weeks and stayed at my auntie's house and other relatives as we visited them. It was a lot different than England; it was so open spaced and cars driving without any traffic controls, no traffic lights and there was cattle walking between them, horns blowing, buses were overcrowded and people sat on top of them. People travelled in horse carriages and also carriages pulled by bicycles. We went in all the different transport and had fun.

I had enjoyed myself and saw lots of different fields with crops growing. I picked a sugar cane and tried some. I was sorry because I didn't ask before I helped myself, but the farmer said it was ok. In one of the houses, as I was walking past, I noticed a hammock in their back garden and I said to myself, I would love to have a hammock in my garden one day when I have a house.

While in India I had lost weight due to being sick and we were to fly back to England. I had met a lot of my parent's family and got to know their background.

Back in England I was in six form education for two years before going onto a youth training scheme in Retail.

My Arranged Marriage

I remember it is a Saturday morning as I'm vacuuming the living room and the phone is ringing; dad has answered the phone.

I turned the vacuum off and hear that he is talking to an uncle. The uncle is talking about marriage. Dad is saying that my older sister is not divorced yet so it's a no.

Then I heard my name mentioned. I'm seventeen and a half doing a youth training scheme in Retail, when it all came about talk of marriage.

Dad was saying there is a man who has come over from India and uncle wanted to arrange a marriage quickly.

When my dad met up with this uncle and others, not sure who they were, but had said that I will be treated well and looked after.

I remember my brothers had met him and I was told he is too old for me. He was described as being tall; well, I thought that tall is ok.

In my mind I was thinking if you don't get me married to this guy there will be another guy in an arranged marriage.

Then I said it out loud. If you don't get me married to this guy, there will be someone else, so I don't care.

Growing up life was strict, so I was thinking if I get married I will have freedom. As an Indian girl, I was told we could wear make-up and have our hair cut only once we were married.

I started getting used to the idea that I was going to get married. I've turned eighteen in May and legally allowed to get married.

The date was announced for the engagement, me, my sister and Mum went to his uncle's house where we meet for the first time.

We meet with his two widowed sisters and his aunt; we had tea and stayed for a while. There wasn't much communication between me and the man who was to be my husband.

I guess I didn't know what to expect, I was naive and gullible to the whole situation.

I remember that he was quiet and he smiled. He was tall and well-built and as for me, I was petite.

They had commented on my nice smile as I was always smiling no matter what the situation was; I guess it was the way I coped.

The day has arrived to get married at the registry office. My wedding outfit, to my surprise, was a red sari with sequins.

The wedding itself was with family and a few friends from school days. When I'm at the registry office in Wolverhampton the reality of it is kicking in and I am not happy at all.

My friends are there, the friend I'm about to share my thoughts with was not even a close friend I said "I can't go through with this; it's not what I want for my life." I look up at the sky and I'm asking if there is anyone out there who can help me - Help Me!!!

It's time to go in, family have taken their seats and I am so scared of what is happening. I see him and he looks different, he has had a haircut and looks stern.

The registry has called us to the front, as I'm standing there, the thoughts running in my head are to tell the registry man that he is an illegal immigrant and I'm having an arranged marriage.

I compose myself, then I turned around to get my Mum's attention, I looked directly at her hoping she will read my looks. I wasn't surprised to get a stern look back. It was a look that I could read and it reads don't you dare. I felt guilty, I turned around and it's time to say the vows.

My word, he didn't even know how to speak English.

What have I done? What have I got myself into? I've done it now, I'm married. Confetti is thrown over us and photos are taken. As for me, always smiling, it masked the cry that was in my heart. With him, my husband, a stranger with no holding of hands.

We go home as there is no party; everything was done to keep him in this country. The next time I would meet my husband would be on the Asian wedding day.

I've continued to do my Retail training and at the centre I tell them that I have got married. I buy them all a drink and a chocolate from the vending machine and to me that was my celebration. The afternoon would finish at 4pm and I would catch the bus home.

On the weekends there was no lying in bed after 9am. Mum would wake me up saying "get up and get ready." It was the norm. After freshening up and having breakfast the housework had to be done. I'd see mum cleaning the kitchen and I would vacuum the upstairs and she'd come up to see if I'm doing it properly. I'm thinking it's the vacuum that is sucking the dust so why do I need to scrub the carpet; it does not make sense, but no arguing with Mum.

The house has been cleaned and then it's time to help with dinner. Now it is dinnertime, Oh my! There is Mum, Me and Manpreet in the kitchen and we are going to have chapatti and vegetable curry. One of us has to make the dough and the other to make the chapatti. On this occasion I wanted to make the chapatti and my sister Manpreet was not having it.

We started to disagree, but as always she got her own way and I had to make the dough. After I made the dough I had a go at her and I had said "why did you have to have a divorce and come back home?" Oops! On saying that my Mum came at me with the rolling pin and I ran laughing up the stairs. I came down the stairs knowing it had calmed down and had to carry on with the dinner.

The day for the wedding was getting nearer and we began to do some clothes and make-up shopping. The clothes I got to buy were traditional and some western trouser and blouses. I had no idea what would be suitable as I was not allowed to wear any. I chose the make-up on knowing the colours I would like.

The wedding dress was a traditional Lengha dress with a head covering which had red and gold sequins. I didn't have a new wedding outfit as this was first worn by my sister and the suitcases I had were also previously used by Manpreet.

In between the engagement and the wedding I didn't see my husband at all.

He would telephone and we would chat about our day. Sometimes we'd be on the phone a while and my dad would not be very pleased. Dad would say "what have you got to talk about?" and I would laugh.

Now the wedding day is near, I have to come out of doing the youth training scheme. I've said my goodbyes to the friends and ready to start a new life.

In a traditional Indian wedding, where it takes three days of celebration, it included having red bangles put on and a paste made with turmeric, which is rubbed on the hands, face, arms and feet by the family and it is done once each day on a Friday and Saturday before the wedding on Sunday.

My pre wedding was different, there were not many guests, the family that was there were my sister and sister in law and a family friend. I wasn't made a fuss of and everything was done quick and unplanned. On the wedding day I've got myself ready, the wedding outfit is on and a friend has done my make-up and I don't like it. The wedding took place at the local temple and then photographs were taken. In the evening the husband came to our house with some of his relatives to take me to start a married life. I had a bet with Ricky that I would not cry when I leave and I didn't, instead I laughed and said goodbye.

In the car I sat in the back with husband Gurjit and a lady from his side of the family and I got unsettled because he started pinching me and I remember the lady giving him a look of despair.

The journey took around forty five minutes to his sister's house where we would be living. When we got there we were greeted by his side of the family; complete strangers to me. Now it's evening and I'm shown to the bedroom where I sleep on my own. The next morning after breakfast, I've been given a sari to wear which they had bought and then we came back to my parent's house where I stayed for a few days as a married woman.

It is time to go back to the marital home and I'll be living with his sister Bashi and her four children. On the night as I get ready for bed I realise that he will be sharing the same bed. Now that I knew it, I got uncomfortable and I didn't like it when he touched me. The family relatives who were staying over spoke to me and said that now I'm married I will be sharing the same bed. They said because I was upset Gurjit will on this night sleep in the other room and his aunt will sleep and stay with me which I agreed. I've even slept well. I'm not sure what to expect as I am a married woman at the age of eighteen and been unsure and naive.

I got dressed in my western clothes and came downstairs, but his sister Bashi said that it would be best if I wore traditional Asian clothes. So I did respect that and I got changed. Now breakfast was already made and I was told to have something to eat, but I didn't like eating as

I would get an upset stomach, I had said I wasn't hungry, but they insisted I ate. In the afternoon Bashi said that all the family will be going to visit their relatives; in the evening myself and husband Gurjit were dropped off at home.

We have the house to ourselves. It's the first time Gurjit and I have been on our own and we talk. In the evening Gurjit goes and gets a drink and he is telling me to drink it and I'm asking what is it? He does not say and puts it to my mouth and it's a clear drink of alcohol and it's neat. I didn't even get to say no when he put it to my mouth and made sure I drank it all. After drinking the clear drink, I had no recollection at all until I woke up the next morning in bed with no clothes on and I am in a lot of pain. I had no idea what has happened.

I still haven't got my head round and its throbbing as I've never drank any alcohol in my life growing up. The family is due to come home so I get ready and go about my day.

Gurjit also has another sister Daljit who has two children. They have come to visit. The children are young ages three and four, a boy and a girl.

When I'm around children I seem to interact with them and become childlike. The house is getting full now as the other sister has come home and she has four children, they are three girls and one boy aged up to ten. It's fun playing with the kids. When I was around the adults of the family I noticed that I act grown up.

It has been a couple of weeks into the marriage and I'm being sick a lot and I find out that I'm pregnant. What? I'm thinking, I'm going to have a baby. What am I supposed to do now? I'm married and pregnant within two weeks of marriage and didn't have a honeymoon. Things are changing now as I've been living here a couple of weeks. Bashi's children attend a school that is a fifteen minutes' walk away and I've been asked to pick them up. It gets tiring with walking there and back and then I have to cook their food. I'm used to cooking fish fingers so they are cooked but Bashi starts to complain about my cooking that I must cook them the way they like it and that was almost looking uncooked, and she didn't care what I had to say and then in the evening I had to cook for the whole family before I got to eat, and then I was too exhausted to eat and just wanted to sleep.

Gurjit would start work early in the morning so I had to get up at six thirty to make his tea and breakfast; when he would go to work I would go back to sleep. Waking up around ten in the morning I would get moaned at for staying in bed when there was housework to be done.

The same routine would happen as the day before, and this time in the evening I wasn't feeling well and I said I'm going to bed early and wouldn't be able to make the dinner. Bashi had made the dinner and sent her daughter to call me down for dinner and I had said I wasn't hungry. Gurjit has come from work and she has made his dinner and from upstairs I can hear that she is talking about me to him and saying that I don't listen and do as I'm told. I'm just lying in bed and crying knowing I've done nothing wrong; I am treated like a servant.

The following day I've started to wear dark eye shadow and nothing is being said, until we went out shopping and meet his other sister Daljit. She starts commenting that the make-up I'm wearing is not suitable. I didn't have a choice; I was masking the bruise I had when Gurjit slapped my face, bruising my eye. The children had noticed that something was up with my eye and but I told them that it was OK.

As time went on I had grown fond of the children, we would enjoy playing in the garden. On one occasion, while we were in the garden, Bashi had opened the bedroom window to see what we were all doing. This is the first time she did this so I was a bit suspicious, so after she had closed the window, I waited a while and told the kids that I was going to the bathroom and will be back so keep playing. As I went back in the house I'm trying my best to be as quiet as

I can as I walked up the stairs to our bedroom. When I enter the bedroom Bashi is there and all of a sudden she starts to say "oh, the windows need a clean" and then walks out of the room. I knew she was up to something. I didn't catch her red handed so I had no evidence that she had been stealing from us. What I did was, when husband Gurjit gave his wages to me, I would put some of the money under the mattress. Later, when I lifted the side of the mattress, the money had gone.

I would tell my husband that I thought Bashi stole the money because I caught her in our bedroom. He would say that there is nothing we can do because we are living under her roof. Money would disappear on many occasions and I would try to hide it in all different places. One time I had twenty pounds in my purse and before we went out for the afternoon I had put my purse in the kitchen, I thought nothing of it. When we were out and about buying some food I opened my purse to find it empty.

I could not believe it, when did I leave my purse unattended. Gurjit kept saying I might have forgotten to bring the money with us, but I knew I had and remembered leaving my purse in the kitchen when I went to the downstairs toilet. So we ended coming back home, keeping quiet.

At home his other sister Daljit and her two kids were there and all they did was moan about how we have money to go out and eat and why we couldn't eat at home. Finally, we decided to have a word with Bashi and mentioned to her that money was going missing. So she told us to start locking the bedroom door and keep the key with us. I knew there was no point in doing that, although we did, money and other items still went missing. She had a spare key which I couldn't prove.

On the weekends Gurjit would decide to go and visit his other sister and her two children, and I would ask if I could go as well. It was a break from here. She lived in a two bedroom flat which we had a room when we visited. Sometimes I would stay more than a few days and then I would be taken advantage of. I had to do the housework and take her kids to school because she went to work. During the day I would be on my own, which I enjoyed having time to myself.

Being pregnant, I was craving a lot of sweets and I'd sit and watch TV, eating as many sweets as I could. All of a sudden there was a knock on the door; I wondered who it could be? I had a peek through the living room door and noticed that his sister Bashi had come; my heart sank. I quickly started to put the sweets away before going to open the door.

She asked why I took so long to answer the door as I invited her in; I had said I was resting. I asked how she was as it takes two buses to get here and over an hour's journey. She wasn't very pleased that we were staying over here and she made it clear. Whilst we were staying at her house we were paying housekeeping and when we stayed here, we would like to pay our way here too.

Bashi had decided that she was going to India and we were to look after her four kids. The weather here was winter and very cold, I'd get the shopping done by travelling on the bus. Bashi had said that she would pay the bills when she came back from India so we would pay and keep the receipts. I would look after the family, the home and had no help from Gurjit. Bashi has been in India for six weeks and due home soon.

Daljit has come over with her two children and that meant more work. All she does is moan to me about how I have spoilt the kids and it will not go well with their mum when she comes back from India. Bashi's back from India now, she asked if everything has been ok. I told her that I had kept all the receipts for the bills we had paid; she replied "you were the ones who used the gas and electricity so why should I pay?"

I'm not happy with my life here and if I got the opportunity I would visit my parent's. I had said to my Mum that I'm not happy in my marriage and I want to come home. She said that I chose to get married and that was my home now. To hear those words broke my heart and that day I died inside myself. I had no choice but to continue in my marriage.

My husband didn't have a permanent stay in this country and unexpectedly, two officers from the immigration office called at the house to interview us. They asked all sorts of questions about our marriage and how we met. Thoughts ran all through my head, if I can tell them the truth about how I'm living here I might get some help, but I remembered saying before I got married that if he got deported I will go and live in India; I didn't mean it though. My own words rang bells.

I told them that I was pregnant and they interviewed Gurjit but as he doesn't speak English; I had to translate.

All his family can think about is him getting his permanent stay. A few weeks later a letter had arrived confirming his stay.

It's the month of July and this morning I kept going to the toilet; Bashi had said the baby may be on its way.

I have phoned the hospital and an ambulance is on its way, even though I had no signs of the baby coming. It was at the hospital that the contractions started and "oh my word what's happening to me?" I'm in so much pain and all I had was a breathing mask to use every time a contraction happened. I gave birth to a baby boy. The first day after the birth the nurses looked after the baby and gave him to me the following morning. I looked at him and my first thoughts were "he's mine" and that he was very light skinned. I was taught how to bath a baby and change nappies, it had come to me so naturally. We came home after a few days and I can remember wanting to sleep all the time as I was exhausted. My clothes would not fit anymore, so they had to be adjusted. My family had come over and blessed my baby with clothes and money. At first I didn't know the Indian traditions of having a baby boy; but I was soon to find out the cost. It was that Indian sweets and traditional suits were given to close family.

Gurjit said that we needed money, but we didn't have the amount that was required. I've got eight hundred pounds in a saving account which I had saved when I did my youth training scheme. So when I came to visit my parents I asked if I can have my savings account book. I didn't tell them why I needed the money. It all got spent on treating other people because of celebrating our baby. I still couldn't get my head round it. Visitors kept coming to visit the baby and would bless the baby with gifts of money and clothes.

One morning as I was about to come downstairs there was a knock on the door so I sat on the top of the stairs. The visitor was giving Bashi a note of money for my baby. As he left I saw Bashi go to her coat and put the money in the pocket and take out a couple of coins. I quickly went back into the bedroom and into bed. I hear footsteps coming up the stairs and as she comes into my bedroom, she says that a visitor came and gave a couple of pounds for the baby.

I was so shocked that I stayed quiet as there was nothing I could have done. If I had said anything it would have caused problems. Money was still going missing and so was clothing.

Now we have our own family, we bought a house, but my belongings are still at Bashi's house; I still had her house key. I've planned to go over when she goes to pick her children up from school. When I get to her house no one is in. I wanted to go and get some of my baby clothing from the bedroom and when I did I found some of them missing. So I decided to go into her bedroom and straight away I saw my stuff on top of her wardrobe which was behind her bed. I climbed onto her bed and put my foot on the headboard to get to the tall wardrobe, as I was getting my belongings down my foot slipped and I fell onto the edge of the bed; before landing on the floor twisting my ankle.

I'm in so much pain as I get back downstairs to my baby who is sleeping in his pram. Bashi is back from school and I confronted her about taking my things. Her response to me was that my stuff is all over the place, how would I know what I've got? Daljit and another aunty are involved now and I'm told to get all our stuff out from her house and if anyone finds out about this I will be in trouble. I'm absolutely devastated; I tell the truth and I'm the one who gets accused of lying.

My ankle is swollen. Gurjit says that he knows an elder who can massage my ankle. We go and visit him and as he looks at my swollen ankle he suggests that it has to be put right. He takes some material and soaks it in oil, telling me to bite down on another cloth as he twists my ankle back in place. I could have screamed, but I didn't. He then wrapped the oiled bandage around my ankle and told me to take it easy and soon it will be ok.

Now Daljit has decided that she wants to move from the flat where she lived, to a house near us. She moved onto the same road as us.

She would have the habit of coming over every day. My baby is a few months old and I'm pregnant again; even though I was wearing a contraceptive coil. I've been to the doctors and have had it confirmed, I asked the doctor "how am I going to cope when my baby is only a few months old?" This pregnancy was normal as I had no sickness and carried it well. I was looking forward to my second baby, when the time was due I remember craving fish and chips which I had and the same evening I was taken to hospital and gave birth to a beautiful baby girl. I was so happy now I have a boy and a girl.

Although Gurjits' sisters were weeping and grumbling that I had a girl because they had too many girls in their family. They were hoping of another boy. Daljit had looked after my boy and I wanted to get home soon. It wasn't easy looking after two children both in nappies; my boy was teething and would have a pacifier.

When Daljit would come over she would complain that he has the pacifier too much and would take it from him and leave him crying. I would be told that it's my fault that I keep giving it to him. I didn't like what was said to me over and over again, but I said nothing.

Gurjit would go to work in the morning and would be back in the evening and not once would he help with feeding or changing the nappies but wanted his meal cooked and to be ready on time when he came back from work.

My baby boy is now eighteen months old and Gurjit wants to visit his parents in India and he wants to take our boy with him.

I'm not very pleased at all and I don't want him to take my baby. Daljit said that she will be going as well and would take care of him. Even though I didn't want him to go I had no say.

They have returned home having been in India for six weeks and I am so happy to see my boy again. Daljit said that he had diarrhoea all the time and that I didn't pack enough nappies and had to use the cloth ones. I said that I did pack a lot of nappies but they took so much luggage with them that a suitcase was rejected and had to come back and that suitcase contained the nappies. But it was still my fault. Nothing ever pleased them.

Gurjit's parents lived in India so he was responsible to providing for them so he would send some of his wages to look after them. He would borrow money off his sister's and we would be in debt to them.

Gurjit wants to start his own business and discusses it with Daljit, so she puts some money his way and he starts to sell clothing on a market stall. Things are not running smoothly and he is having difficulty managing the stall as it's not bringing in a proper income. We are in debt now and he has to go back to work. His father wants to come over from India to visit and the money is borrowed to buy the ticket.

Gurjit had some cousins who had bought a newsagent shop and as they sold a variety of birthday cards and other cards they didn't know the order that they are put, so they asked Gurjit and Daljit if I would be able to help them. When Gurjit mentioned it to me I had said that I would like to help them, when would they want the help?

Gurjit snapped at me and said who do they think they are asking for your help and then Daljit also joined in and said that when they come over to our house and ask me to help them I am to refuse and say I don't have the time. I did what I was told and I felt so uncomfortable.

So when we were invited to visit them at their shop, they were lovely people and spoke to Gurjit and Daljit blanking me out. I was so dismayed; if only they knew the truth. Whilst I was in their shop I asked if I could help, their response was that I never helped when they needed it and now they don't need my help. After that visit months had passed and then we visited again. It was years later when I told them the truth.

I've taken some pictures of my toddlers during the summer in the garden and one of the pictures I had enlarged. I needed a picture frame and I chose a frame which already had a picture in it. The picture was of Jesus and I had put my children's picture on top of it and in my heart I would say that Jesus will look after my children and keep them protected. I didn't know why I did that as I was a Sikh and we worshipped Gurus. I did remember though when I was at school we always had an assembly every morning and sang hymns to the Lord and finishing with Amen.

Gurjit's dad has arrived in the UK and will be staying with us. I would describe him as a pleasant man. He plays a little with his grandchildren as they get to know him. In the evening he would go to rest early and in the morning he would like his breakfast in bed. That had become a routine which I was ok with. Sometimes he would stay with his daughter who lived down the road. I enjoyed his company and when I did the shopping father-in-law would go with me.

Gurjit is going to India for six weeks to visit his mum and while he is away I have received an appointment to have an operation for a blocked nose, which I suffered with from childhood. After the operation I was so emotional and in pain that I struggled to look after myself, the kids and making father-in-law breakfast.

Daljit comes over to visit and asks what is wrong, but I'm not close enough to her to share my heart as all they have done to me is cause grief. I've spoken to my mum on the phone and she has suggested coming over there and having some rest. I've asked my father-in-law if it would be ok to stay with my mum for a while. He said it would be a good idea if I waited until Gurjit came back from India.

 I struggled and carried on with life being unhappy. When my husband came back from India I asked him if I could go and stay at my Mum's for a while and he asked why I didn't go whilst he was in India. I'm not allowed to go now.

It's been two years now since the father-in-law has been staying with us and the mother-in-law has come over to this country to visit. I do my best to make her feel welcome; I still do all the cooking and look after the kids. She spends a lot of time with her daughters and always seems cold towards me. Money is tight as only one income is coming in and she suggests that, while she is here, that I get a job and she will look after the children.

An aunty, who works at a sewing factory, had said there was a vacancy as a receptionist. So I applied for the position and got the part-time job. I would miss the kids a lot and when I would get home it was a right mess and their grandparents would say these kids don't listen to us but behave well when I'm here. My daughter was teething at the time and bit her grandmother on the leg and when I got to know about it, which was days later, I had been accused of telling my daughter to bite her leg by sister-in-law Daljit. I had to defend myself and had said "how can I tell a little girl to do that? It's not true."

The factory that I worked for was Asian-owned and it was on an estate with other factories and I knew one of the clients who would visit as another factory owner.

A few weeks into the job a phone call came to me as I'm the receptionist, it was my husband. He said "I know what you go to work for and I want you to come home right now?" He was angry and scaring me, what am I going to be been accused of this time? I thought.

Leaving work there were some lads outside the factory playing football and as I was walking the ball came to me, not thinking anything of it I had kicked the ball back to them. It took me a while to get home as I waited for a bus. Even then when I got home, I was questioned as to why I was late. My husband and his mum were in the house with the kids and I'm asking them what has happened? His mum had her mouth covered with her shawl and giving me the stare of cold eyes and Gurjit says "you know what you have been doing," I had no idea and I asked mum "What happened? What is going on?" She is accusing me of having an affair. I could not believe what I was hearing and have been accused of.

No way! I said, I would never do that. My husband had said "I know but that's my mum." I've been accused of having an affair and I'm asking his mum when all this allegedly took place. She is saying that it was when Gurjit was doing night shifts; that was weeks ago. I asked her why she did not say it then. Why now? I asked. Where did it all take place? "In this house" she said when Gurjit was doing night shifts and she was supposed to be asleep upstairs. She said that she heard voices downstairs and came onto the upper landing and saw a shadow on the wall. I said "why didn't you come downstairs then?" Her reply was "because you both might have killed me".

Oh my, what next? I told her that it was the television that was on and I was putting the lock on the door before I came up to bed to be with my children. In that moment, everything got heated up so I rang my Dad and told him what I was being accused of.

Then, within the hour, Dad and Ricky came over and saw me so distressed and tried to calm the situation.

Dad and Ricky were going back home and I said that I was going to stay upstairs and not be in the same room as them. Dad then said it would be better if I came home with him. I refused to go and said I will be ok here. The place felt as if fireworks had exploded. My father-in-law said "I've lived here two years and nothing has ever happened." He was taking my side and the arguing got worse.

They were ready to hit me, when I said that if any of you lay a hand on me I will call the police. Mother-in-law then said "don't touch her." Daljit then said "oh you've got a mouth haven't you?" and their mother said that she wasn't staying with us and was not going to look after the children and went to stay with her other daughter Bashi. Gurjit used to drink alcohol and his father did too, it was constant drinking. I would fear for the safety of our children and would keep them away from him. I sometimes even feared for my own safety and would lock myself in the bathroom at times.

He would say that "if I wanted to, I can break the door down and smash your face." I would be so tensed up and then come out calmly. I'm struggling to cope. Gurjit had been drinking heavily through the night and he abused me. In the morning as he was going to work, he even asked me if I was OK. When he had gone to work I started to overdose on tablets. I didn't know what else to do. I wanted the pain to go away. So I rang the doctor and told her what I had done.

Manpreet rang that day and I was now feeling drowsy, she asked what was wrong, I told her and soon she had turned up with Paul. They took me to the hospital with the kids and afterwards we went to Paul's house; where we stayed for many weeks. I don't know why I couldn't stay at my mum's. I wasn't happy staying at Paul's as it felt so isolated.

As weeks went by, I had no money so I had applied for benefit for myself and my children. That took a long time.

By the time I started to receive the benefit I had gone back to my marital home and didn't even get any.

In my heart, I wanted to run away, but was too scared and didn't know how to go about it. Now Gurjit had been talking to Paul and said that we needed to sort this out. I was so afraid and as I didn't see any way out, I said that I will go back. His mum and dad came to visit my parents to take me back; but I refused to go with them.

It was when Gurjit came to get me that I went back to the martial home with the children. I didn't see any change in our marriage; it was full of arguing and he was complaining as to why I didn't come home when his parents went to get me and how I had insulted them by not coming home with them. I would still cook for the whole family; even though they were giving me the silent treatment and kept making me feel uncomfortable.

Gurjit's mum and dad were soon to go back to India and things haven't got much better. We were getting into more debt and Gurjit was drinking even more alcohol and had now started gambling. He was borrowing money off Daljit and Bashi to buy his parents tickets and a ticket for himself to go to India.

I was always depressed and kept being sick. After many tests it was revealed that I had an allergy to gluten. I didn't find that very easy to adjust to because it meant that I would be making my meals separate using gluten free flour.

While Gurjit was away, his sister Bashi would come round and help with doing the shopping, on this occasion I had some money that I was counting in front of Bashi and she asked if she could have a hundred pounds as she needed it.

I gave it to her and she said that we could take it off the amount that we owed.

The night before it had been snowing and it had settled on the ground. As we were leaving the house I had noticed footprints in the snow in our small front garden. I just thought that someone might have been looking through our window, but I didn't think anything of it. We went shopping and on the way home, we met a lady who said "I've been knocking on your door and there was no answer."

We were about ten minutes away from home and when we got to my house the front door was open. I called out to see if there was anyone there; I was scared to go in so we asked the neighbour to call the police asking her if she had heard or seen anyone enter our house through the back garden, she replied no. When the police arrived I followed them in the house keeping behind them. Everything downstairs was ok, although the bathroom window had been broken into and when we went upstairs we found tools that were left as they tried to open the safe.

The police asked me if I was ok staying on my own and I said yes. During that evening I was so scared that I got the kids to bed and then hid myself in the bed covers until I fell asleep. The feeling was horrible knowing someone had been here.

Gurjit is gambling more and more and many times he won a large amount of money, which he would start to pay back his sister's. I had told him that Bashi had a hundred pounds from me and when he asked her she had totally denied it and said that she offered me money. I couldn't believe it; also I had no proof.

I'm pregnant again and its four years after my daughter was born. This pleased me because I had a break. Gurjit drank, as always, and complained about me being pregnant now and not when his parents were here. I didn't want that and would tell him that I couldn't cope with another baby at the moment. I would have a baby in a few years, when Michael and Sarah have grown up.

As I'm cooking the evening dinner Gurjit said he was going to get a video to watch and would be gone about fifteen minutes, it had been an hour since he left; when there was a knock on the front door. When I answered the door, his sister Daljit was standing there and said "a man came knocking on your door earlier, why didn't you open it? He had to come and knock on my door to tell me what has happened". I didn't hear the door knock because I was cooking and couldn't hear the door through the other doors, which were shut. Why, what has happened? I asked, and she told me that Gurjit had been hit by a car as he was crossing the road and has been taken to hospital. Daljit suggested that, because I'm pregnant, I should stay at home and she and Bashi would go to the hospital instead. I've had no phone call and I was getting tired, so when I put the kids to bed, I had a lay down with them and fell asleep. I woke up at midnight, startled, as I heard banging on the front door. I woke myself and went downstairs to answer the door, it was Bashi. She said "is that all you can think about is sleep when Gurjit is in hospital?" I replied that I was waiting for news and fell asleep, what else could I do? I'm pregnant. She looked at me sternly before going back home. Gurjit stayed in hospital for a week before he was discharged. When I would visit him he would moan, then he would tell me not to come again without food as he didn't like the food here.

When my baby is born it was a boy. It's been a few months now and we've decided to move.

Living here for about seven years and the house prices had started to rise up and as we didn't get to a great start, we decided we were going to move house and live in another town. Paul helped look for another house with Gurjit, and when a house was bought I was not included and I only saw it when we moved in.

I liked the house, it had three bedrooms, a large garden and a school located at the back of the garden. I loved doing DIY, I would do the wallpapering and painting and also do the gardening. Gurjit would work and continued to drink alcohol and gamble in the casinos.

It had become a habit. His cousins would travel to visit us only to moan and complain about how far they have to travel. When they had left I would be in trouble again and be blamed for all the problems we had. Gurjit would say it's entirely my fault for bringing shame on the family. He would then start drinking more alcohol, swearing and then expect me to feed him his dinner.

One weekend we were going to visit my parents and I'm excited that I was going to wear the gold necklace my dad had bought me, which I looked after. I even forgot what it looked like. When I had put the necklace on it looked dull in colour and I told my husband that I was going to tell dad about the necklace and ask him to take it back to the jewellery shop where he had bought it from. He then said to me "you stupid woman, don't you realise that it is a fake?" What do you mean? I asked, "I've sold your necklace and in its place I put this fake one." I couldn't believe what I was hearing and I burst out crying asking him why? He wasn't having any of it and I told him that I wasn't going now. I didn't have a choice, I still had to go and visit and act as if everything was OK.

His sister's would come over and visit and moan about the length of the journey too. They would see my baby boy and comment how he doesn't look like his dad. They just loved causing friction in our marriage. That would fuel him even more and when he'd been drinking he would say that our baby doesn't look like him and ask whose he was? I would be fuming and I would say at "least I know he is mine." I didn't care anymore as I had got used to him hitting me, as long as I was keeping my children safe from him when he was drunk. He would apologise though; when he was sober.

Even though he spent money on alcohol and gambling, I was the one to manage the household bills and I always made sure the bills were paid and that we had food on the table. Over time I had managed to save seven hundred pounds, which was on a joint saving account. I had hidden the account book under a trunk which I had. One day he asked me if his cousin could borrow seven hundred pounds and asked me if I would lend it to him. No! I replied, because that's our savings. He laughed in my face and said that he already took it and gambled it. No way! I said, because you don't know where the book is. He described to me exactly where it was. Again, I had to pick myself up and live for my children. My baby boy is six weeks old now and Gurjit came home drunk and as always, demanding his own way. I don't like it when he is drunk as he gets violent and wants to be with me but I have refused. He doesn't take no for an answer and violently forces himself on me. Later in the night I take a lot of pain killers to numb the pain and in the morning he is apologising again.

Weeks later I find out that I'm pregnant and in no way am I able to cope with this. I've been making enquiries about having an abortion and they asked a lot of questions. I told them that the contraceptive was faulty.

I did not know what to do as I had no one to turn to for help. Everything I did or didn't do turned out to be my fault. I am not able to cope with another child; so I decided to have an abortion. I asked Ruby if she would look after my children for the day as I told her I have an appointment to attend to and will be away for the night.

I would now be constantly accused of being a murderer by my husband, after his drinking. I was so hurt inside that I would lash out and accuse him of raping me and how I couldn't raise another child.

A day wouldn't go by when I didn't think about the baby. I would remember how old the baby would be each day. I would pray and say to God that I was sorry and would ask Him to look after my baby. I struggled for many weeks but I focused on the children I did have. Two of my children went to the school that was located behind the garden. At their playing time they would come to the fence and shout for me, I would then go to the back of the garden with ice lollies 'tip tops' as the weather was warm; the youngest child was at home with me.

I had good neighbours, they were an elderly couple Fred and Wendy. Fred enjoyed gardening and whenever Fred was in the garden we would chat over the small garden fence. He would give me tips on gardening and also give me some flowers to plant. Fred enjoyed Indian food, so when I cooked curries, I would plate some up and put it on a tray and call out to Fred over the garden fence. He would see me through his dining room window and wave. He would come into the garden and enjoy the meal and sit on his garden bench; his wife didn't like curries. He would say that I was a great cook and even though he had already eaten; he would always enjoy my food.

Fred would spend most of his time in the garden, as I was a housewife, I would enjoy talking with Fred as he was the closest person I had to talk to.

He knew something was wrong with me, although he would never pry in my business, but this time he did say that I looked like I was going to die, as I was looking so pale.

I would say that I've not been well and that I will be ok. I would never share my true feelings. I was always afraid of my husband and didn't want anything getting back to him. Wendy would come out into the garden when she would hang out the washing and then have a chat; otherwise she kept herself indoors.

Fred has been unwell for a while now and I've missed his company.

When his family would come to visit, I would be asking how he is. They would pass the message on. All of a sudden he was getting worse and not any better. Weeks went by and then I had a knock on the door and it was his granddaughter. I was hoping she had come round to say Fred is a lot better now, but the look on her face was saying something else. I asked how Fred was. It was very sad for me to hear her say that Fred had passed away. He had been a very dear friend to me and I was hoping to say goodbye but it never happened.

I was so upset. I hoped to be at his funeral and see the coffin when it arrived at the house. I didn't know the day of the funeral and I wasn't invited. I saw Wendy a few weeks later in the garden and I asked about the funeral and when it would be taking place? She had said it had already happened and how well it all went and asked me where I was. I remember on that day I had been to visit my mum. I was shocked. I came into the house and cried and cried. About how I missed the friend I once had. As time went by, when I would be in the garden, I would hear Wendy go into her garden; then I would go back indoors.

I would be doing it constantly and at times I would say to her "I'm so busy that I've got so much house work to do." I was finding it difficult to cope with Fred passing away and not being invited to the funeral. One night in my sleep I had a dream, I had seen Fred standing on a bridge, which had steps, and he was waving to me. I sat up in bed and cried and waved to him. I got to say my goodbye. I saw him walk away until he was out of view. I remembered my dream in the morning and it felt so real.

I've decided to go and visit Wendy as her daughter has come to visit.

I've also taken a bunch of flowers with me and I said that I wanted to explain my behaviour. I'm telling them how I missed Fred and that I didn't get to say goodbye as I wasn't invited to the funeral. On hearing what I had said, they were so apologetic and they both thought I was told about the funeral and they said how Fred was very fond of me and always spoke highly of me.

Wendy was saying how Fred would say that I deserved better. As Wendy now lived on her own I would visit and see if I could help in any way, this time she was not feeling well and I asked her if I could pray with her and she loved it, I was surprised with her reply as she said "Baljit, God is with you." I would help Wendy if she needed any shopping and spend time talking over the garden. She was a lovely lady and sadly had passed away. We had known each other for twenty years. They were the best neighbours.

The first time I ever read a bible was when my son Michael was in junior school, he brought home a New Testament, a little red book and he gave it to me. Inside it had so many scriptures and numbers relating to worldly life. I would look up the numbers that I would see about my life and it would go to a scripture. As I read the verse 'feeling lost' it read in Luke 19:10 *'For the Son of man is come to seek and to save that which was lost.'*

I didn't have the understanding of it as it was the opposite of what I thought. How can that be? I would come back later and read more. I'd go and find a verse on 'being attacked' and it was in Psalm 35:1-2 *'Plead my cause, O Lord, with them that strive with me: fight against them that fight against me. Take hold of shield and buckler, and stand up for mine help.'*

Then another Psalm 32:8 read *'I will instruct thee and teach thee in the way which thou shalt go: I will guide thee with mine eye.'* Now that made sense. Was it God talking to me?

I've put the bible away and didn't tell my husband about it as I didn't want to get in trouble; all he was interested in was alcohol and making money by gambling.

He would at times say that he is going to change and I would have hope and believe him. It's a sunny day and our children are asking if they could go to the park. Gurjit is sober, so he takes them to the local park while I did the cooking. It's been a few hours when they come home. I was shocked to hear what had happened; I'm shouting at him and saying "how could you put my children in danger when you have said you would change?"

I was in such a rage that my thoughts were racing as to what could have happened? I held it together, he replied "nothing happened" and threw it back at me. What had happened was that they had come back home in a stranger's car. The man spoke to me and explained that he saw this man falling all over the place with three children who were flagging down cars to get help. He stopped as he lived nearby and asked if he could help; he saw Gurjit was drunk.

The children gave this man our home address and he drove them here. I thanked the man. I spoke to my children asking them if they were OK and to tell me their side of the story. As I spoke to them, they said they were scared and at first a guy came running from the chip shop to help Gurjit up onto his feet. Then they knocked on someone's door asking to use their telephone to ring home and said to me "but you didn't answer." They described their dad falling all over the place.

Now that our children are all in full time education I am thinking of working. I even asked my husband if I could work, his first question was "how do I know you would not bring disgrace on my family again?" I replied "I never did." I was falsely accused and had to live with it.

Starting Work

It is now 1995, a new factory has opened and I am interested in working there. It's been more than 10 years since I last worked, as I've been a homemaker; looking after three children and a husband which was a full time job in itself.

I remember having to go through a long interview process, literally interview after interview; it also had a practical test.

I passed the entire test and the interviews were successful and therefore I will be starting work on a three shift basis.

It's a food factory so I'm right at home, working in the ingredients department. All training is being given and I'm very enthusiastic and full of excitement to be working.

The first time I met Dave was when I started working at Sun Valley, as it was a new factory that had opened, the team had to go on a training course in Hereford for two weeks;

accommodation and meals were provided for. At the end of the working day we all went to the hotel, at the time we went for our evening meal; there were not many places left to sit.

I noticed that there were a couple of spaces where Dave was sitting so I asked if it was ok to join them on his table. At the time I didn't know Dave was an engineer and so were the others sitting at the table.

 There was another woman sitting at the table and Dave was sitting between us both. The other guys were commenting to Dave how he was like the thorn between two roses. That was the first time I ever met Dave and inside me it felt as if I had already known him. That was the only time in Hereford I saw Dave.

At Sun Valley I'd be working shifts, Dave happened to be the engineer on the same shift. As time went by we would talk more and more. Once, when I was working in the dry ingredients room, I would hear a whistle in the corridor, straight away I would know that it was Dave. I would giggle and when Dave came into the dry ingredients room I would ask him for help in pouring the bags of rice in the trays as they weighed 25kg each, he was a gentleman and helped me out; even though he said he had his own work to do.

At break times we would all sit around the same table having meals and I would notice that Dave didn't talk very much; I saw him as a reserved person.

It has been a couple of years since I've worked at Sun Valley and I would talk to Dave a lot. Many others didn't understand Dave but I enjoyed talking with him. He was married and he never spoke about his marriage; as I did. I saw Dave as my best friend. I could talk to him about anything I wanted and he never judged me, he knew everything about me and yet I didn't know much about him; apart from that he was married with two children and his daughter worked at the same place.

The challenge of work starts to unfold; I had a shift plan, a husband, three children and a home to look after.

Afternoon shift started at 2pm until 10pm for 5 days, this was followed by a night shift from 10pm until 6am and then a morning shift of 6am to 2pm.

I so looked forward to working and I'd work hard knowing I would be able to bring in an income and do up the house.

Each shift had its own challenges with home life. When it was the afternoon shift I would have to wake up at 4.30 every morning.

I'd have my prayer time in my closet, which was the under-stair cupboard. I was seeking God so I worshipped all Gods. I would read a scripture from the bible as well. That would take me about half an hour to forty five minutes.

Then I'd make my husband his breakfast of boiled eggs and a cup of tea and take it upstairs to him; then make his lunch so he can take it to work. It was now time to wake the children. They have their breakfast and then get ready for school. After I've seen them off to school and had my breakfast, I am planning the day.

I've got to be at work by 1.30 pm. I have to make the evening dinner for my children and my husband.

I usually made a curry with chapatti and then Gurjit would serve the kids and himself after work. I'd get back from work after 10pm and our kids would be in bed.

I got home after this shift and as I put the key in the front door, I was greeted by Gurjit; he slaps me across the face. He had been drinking and told me that I didn't make enough chapatti, "I'm so sorry I didn't make extra" I said. He said that I make him so angry that he has to keep me in my place and that he is the only one that will ever love me and no else will ever have me.

He would say that he could get married again if he wanted, but he wouldn't do that. He would say that I could leave him but the children are his and they wouldn't be allowed to go with me. Where would I go? I would stay because of my love for my children.

Across the road from our home was a corner shop where Gurjit would buy alcohol. Even if he didn't have any money they would put it on a tab for him. When I would go in to buy the kids some sweets; it was made known that he had a tab. I would end up having to pay and I even asked them not to serve him any alcohol. I knew I would be in trouble, but I had to try. Gurjit found out and lashed out at me. He said he'll get alcohol from elsewhere and I had to correct my errors with the shop.

Now that I was working I would still manage the finances and always made sure that the bills were paid. I also managed to get some work done on the house.

At times, when I couldn't go to pay the bills, I would ask Gurjit to pay and I would give him the correct amount of money for each bill.

It was the mortgage payment of two hundred and twenty pounds, which needed to be paid. He hasn't come home all day and now it's evening. When he got home, he is in a mess, I ask him what happened? Gurjit said that he got into town late and the building society closed so he didn't make a payment. That didn't explain why he was upset. He went on to say that he got mugged on the way home and they stole the money. I believed him and said that we should call the police. He refused and said he didn't see who they were or be able to describe them. I asked then, "Why didn't they steal your wedding ring?" He had an answer for everything; "I put it in my sock" he said.

Over time bills started coming in red letters and I would follow it up and tell them that I had paid them.

I'm changing the bedding in the children's room and as I lift up the mattress to fold in the sheet; I see all the unpaid bills piled up. Oh My God! What has he done? When Gurjit gets back from work I asked him why is he doing this. "Isn't it enough that I'm working now and looking after the family and you're still behaving like this, when you have said that you would change?"

Gurjit said that he had tried but went to the casino hoping he could make more money. He was winning and even cashed it out, he thought he could win some more and gambled it all. Then he needed more money to win back what he had lost.

Also he confessed that when the mortgage payment was to be made, he lied about being mugged and spent the money at the casino. Same as always he would say he was sorry and that he would stop drinking and gambling. I kept hoping it would come true. Every morning I would get up and pray, asking the Gods to help me to become stronger and that one day I would be happy and my children will have a better future. I would also read a verse from the red Bible; I saw it as a gift from my son.

Night shifts were easier as I could see my children to school and be with them after school and even at bedtimes. The shift would start at ten in the evening until six in the morning. I would work between the two departments called the wet and dry ingredients. We all worked as a team. One person I got talking to lived only a few roads away from me and we decided to travel in a car together. I would pick up Baljinder and drop her off after every shift. She offered some money for the travelling but I said it was ok as I was going almost the same route.

I didn't have the best of cars, as Baljinder would say; she knows when I'm coming as the car made so much noise. I would say it is doing well because it's getting us to work and back. Baljinder and I got on well and worked well together. She did have a habit of pinching my arm if things didn't go her way. This one time I told her "stop pinching my arm as I'm getting annoyed with you." She didn't stop and thought it was funny to keeping winding me up. At the time I was weighing some wet ingredients and I said to her "if you keep on doing it you'll be wearing this vinegar." She found it funny and went back to work in the dry ingredients room. A little later we were chatting and she'd pinch me again. I had a bucket of vinegar nearby so I got the bucket and threw the vinegar at her and told her that she would wear it if she didn't stop. The others laughed so much and didn't think I had it in me to do it. I now had to clean the mess and Baljinder just moaned and said I had ruined her top. Well, it worked because she stopped her habit of pinching.

On the weekend we had a wedding to attend and all of us have been invited. While we were at the wedding hall, our car lock was being picked at. I noticed it when we were leaving the party and I couldn't get in the car through the driver's side; so I went through the passenger's side. Gurjit was drunk again and as I'm driving home, I drove over a bridge, then the car on the other side crashes into our car but doesn't stop and drives off. I braked so hard to stop the car going over the embankment that the bumper goes flying in the air.

I was getting out of the car checking that everyone was ok and asking people walking by at the time if they were ok. The police have arrived and asked me to come into their car. They questioned me about the accident and also expressed a concern about my husband's behaviour asking if I was ok?

Passersby reported what they saw and said the other car was going too fast. Later in the day the other car was found abandoned. The driver of the other car had also been attending the same wedding we went to. He had been drinking and driving.

Now going back to work I had no car and Baljinder didn't drive. Her husband suggested that he would buy her a small car and said that I could keep the car at my house, pick up Baljinder for work and use the car whenever I needed to. That worked well as I didn't charge Baljinder for taking her to work and I didn't pay anything towards the car.

It is now my night shift week and Gurjit has said that he will take the children out for the day. He is going to take them to Dudley zoo and travel by bus. I thought that's nice and I'll be able to have a lie in. It's about one in the afternoon when I got a phone call; it was my older son Michael. "Mum, Dad has left us here and gone into the pub." I'm still sleepy and getting my head round asking where are you? What's going on? Stay all together where you are! I've phoned Daljit and told her what is happening.

We were all concerned now, finally Gurjit comes home with the children and finds out that Michael had told me what had happened and that I had told Gurjit's sister about what he has done. He shouts at Michael and goes to hit him, but I get in the way to protect him. I shouted to Gurjit to leave my boy alone so I got slapped. After constant arguing it's time for my night shift. All the time at work I would have my children on my mind and other workers would say that it looked like I had the world on my shoulders.

I would laugh it off and carry on with my work, as I would always have a smile on my face but with a deep hidden secret; in my heart I was living a life of hell. I was searching for God, who is he? Where would I find him? One of the workers I worked with was a Christian and he would talk to me about Jesus, he even gave me a youth Bible but I still didn't understand who God was. At home, in my prayer room, I had different pictures of Gods. I would pray to them all and ask them to help me and my family, I read my little red Bible as well. I would light an Indian candle which was made from pure butter with a wick. I would also light a scented stick also for the Gods. I was in deep search and my hunger for God grew and grew, but I felt no relief. One of my neighbours worshipped Hindu gods; so I worshipped them too. I had heard that it takes a lot of prayers and work before you get to hear from God.

I was desperate and I was willing to do whatever it takes. I would fast on certain days and not eat meat on other days. It also became my sanctuary when Gurjit would be drinking. I would go into my prayer room and I wouldn't be bothered. I would tell the Gods my problems and would wait for answers. At first I would read the Bible then chant to different Gods with my beaded necklace, after many weeks I read the bible last but I couldn't understand why?

Did the Gods not like the bible? I would wake up in the early hours of the morning and meditate for hours before seeing the children to school.

We've been looking to buy a car and my older brother Larry knows about cars. I went to the auctions with him and bought a Vauxhall Cavalier. It was a reliable car and drove well. It had a radio with an aerial which didn't work properly so I was hoping to get an electric aerial fitted.

At work I had a few weeks holiday to take and Gurjit had planned for the whole family to visit his parents in India. I was very reluctant to go and questioned it a lot. He was so convincing that the holiday would do us all good and that he wouldn't drink. We would visit different temples and the children would enjoy the open space and meet other family members. Gurjit planned to go ahead of us with his sister Daljit and said everything would be ready for us when we got there. Deep thoughts in my heart were more about running away with my children and starting a new life without him, so I was thinking where I could run to with them? I had no clue, so we were set to go to India.

I have asked Baljinder's husband if he can get an electric aerial to put on my car whilst I'm away and to keep the car with him until we get back.

The journey to India was enjoyable as the kids enjoyed the flight experience. When we had arrived, Gurjit with his dad and sister came to pick us up. I couldn't see the point of it all because we had less space in the vehicle to travel; it was so cramped. My children wanted to sleep because the journey took eight hours from the airport to the village.

A few days in, I wanted to come home so much that I cried and cried. He was drinking, the food was different and we had to boil all the water we used. I was sick with a stomach bug but still had to look after myself as Gurjit would stay on the farm while I was sick. The children however, enjoyed themselves; that was a joy to me.

We had stayed six weeks and were due to go back to England. On the plane Michael was playing with a toy gun so Gurjit took it off him and put it in his pocket. When we got off the plane and went through security, the alarm bells started ringing; Gurjit was arrested. I was told to carry on with the children and he would be questioned. Before we left the airport, he was released and the toy gun was handed back to him. The officer even gave him a couple of batteries for it. I found that so funny that it was the whole joy of the journey.

Normal life now and it's back to work for us and back at school for the children. I now have an electric aerial in the car and was driving the car when I noticed smoke appearing from the dashboard. I rang Baljinder, who mentioned it to her husband; he said nothing happened when he had the car. He said that he would have a look, but then gave it back to me as he could find nothing wrong. The next day Baljinder and I had been to work. After I had dropped her off home and drove round the corner, I noticed the smoke again so I drove back to her house and knocked on her door.

As I went into her house, she also noticed the smoke, then we saw flames and had to call the fire brigade. Within a few minutes the car was in full flame and the fire brigade had to rip the car apart to put out the fire. The fire was started by an electrical fault. I thanked God that I wasn't in the car for another second. It's back to the auction again and we have bought another cavalier as I had got used to driving them.

The routine was the same each shift I would pick up Baljinder and go to work. It's five thirty in the morning and it was still quite dark, we were chatting away until I noticed a car that was driving too close to mine, I put my foot on the gas a bit more to get away when all of a sudden blue lights were flashing in my mirror and I pulled up and stopped. A policeman came to my car and I put the window down a little, he asked me where we were going at that time of the morning? The first thing I said was you scared me; you could have been anybody, so I put my foot down. He apologised and I told him that we were going to work, he checked out my car and everything added up. We had a good laugh about it at work.

I enjoyed my work and everyday was different, some days were much busier than other days. This one particular day was very busy and corners were being cut. I was asked to help manually pour out a drum of chopped tomatoes into a dolly bin; its weight was two hundred kilograms. While I was helping to lift the drum I heard a crack come from my spine; my other colleagues heard it too. I didn't think anything at the time so I carried on working until I started getting dizzy.

 I went and reported the incident to the shift manager. He asked if I would still be able to carry on working and I said yes. As I continued to work for a while I felt myself slipping and remember holding onto the work surface and telling my work colleagues to help me as I feel like I'm falling; I then collapsed.

When I came around again I saw that a group of work colleagues were standing around me watching; but not doing anything to help me. Dave came to see what was going on and asked them to move out of the way, as he was a first aider he picked me up and took me to the office. An ambulance was called and when they came to the department where I was, their response was "I'm not surprised she collapsed the smell is overpowering," then they went.

Another work colleague was then asked to take me home in a taxi. I went to the doctor's the next day and was put on painkillers and was off work for six weeks. The pain still hadn't gone away and my employer was asking if I would be coming back to work soon.

I have got a note from the doctors to do light duties only. At work we had a nurse who sent me to have weeks of physiotherapy. Weeks and then months were passing by and I was still in pain, I was struggling to cope with work and home life.

I would be very emotional and it showed in my work. I was offered private counselling treatment for six weeks, which I accepted. The counsellor said to me that I must be an asset for the company because they had sent me. The built up pressure from work and family life was getting overwhelming. As I was struggling each day, my employer offered me a part-time contract which I accepted.

At home, I am praying more and more, asking the Gods to help me. I'm looking in my red Bible for a scripture on illness or pain and it is written in Psalm 103:1-4 *'Bless the Lord, O my soul: and all that is within me, bless his holy name. Bless the Lord, O my soul, and forget not all his benefits: Who forgiveth all thine iniquities who healeth all thy diseases; who redeemeth thy life from destruction; who crowneth thee with lovingkindness and tender mercies.'*

I'm still not understanding the meaning of it all though. When I worshipped and meditated on the other Gods I would empty my mind and chant; I would use a beaded necklace. I then would read the Bible which said different. The Bible was saying the way to meditate was to focus on thoughts of the word and reflect on it, pondering over it, also memorising and praying about it.

Work was different now as I worked part-time, and was in a different department with new work colleagues. I would see some of my other mates at break times and I would also see Dave and have our talks.

It is December of year 1999 and we had been invited to Larry and Ruby's house. I have told Gurjit that me and the kids are going to their house and asked if he wanted to come too, but looking at his state, he had been drinking. I had said it is best that he stayed at home and we will be back in the evening. We enjoyed our time there, but all the time whilst I was there I kept thinking about him at home and what state he would be in.

We had gone there by taxi and Ruby and her daughter dropped us at home around about ten in the evening and I asked Ruby's daughter if she would see us into the house which she did and he was not downstairs. After she went I looked around the downstairs and saw masses of something that looked like tobacco in the living room. I've never seen him smoke so it was different. I was feeling unsettled inside and afraid as I didn't know what to expect. I saw the children to bed and went to our room and he was asleep. I tried to be as quiet as possible and got ready for bed.

As I got into bed, he had woken up; I could smell alcohol and fags. All of a sudden he raised his voice and started shouting at me and saying "How could you go without me? Who gave you permission to go? Who do you think you are? Who does your family think they are?" It was then I spoke, I said "I have never spoken against your family so why are you speaking against mine as we only went for the evening."

Gurjit is so angry that he said "I'm going to sort you out." I had slept on the left side of the bed and he slept on the right, so he had grabbed my hair with his left hand and was reaching over his side of the bed to pick up a broken hockey stick; which he kept on his side of the bed. He was stretching so far that I pulled myself from him and fell off the bed where I had left an iron; I fell on the plug. I screamed in pain as I quickly got up and ran down the stairs.

The phone was in the hallway on the window sill, I dialled 999 and asked for help and then ran out the house banging on the neighbour's door; asking for help until the police arrive. It's almost midnight and the police are here and one officer is talking with me and two other officers go to the house where my son has opened the door to them.

All we can hear is Gurjit arguing with the police and he tries to attack them. He gets arrested and is put in the back of the police car.

I was so terrified that I was hiding behind the police officer as we went to the house.

Gurjit was shouting at me from the police car saying that he will get me when he comes out. The police asked if there was someone they could call and I gave them Larry's number. Ruby has come round and suspected something was wrong when we were around their house; about me being unsettled. I've got the kids up and then we all went with Ruby to stay the night.

Waking up in the morning I noticed my left leg was severely bruised and remembered falling on the plug. Thoughts are pounding in my head; I'm feeling so ashamed, What has happened? What have I done; What am I going to do now? Am I in more trouble? Now I'm more terrified. I'm hearing voices downstairs and then hear them coming upstairs, there's a knock on the bedroom door and Gurjit's sister Daljit is there.

I'm taken back and she starts questioning me about what has happened and then she accuses me of causing it.

I couldn't believe what I was hearing but I was so used to them treating me the way they did even I thought it to be right.

It is my night shift and I'm due to be at work, Ruby said she would look after the children so I could go to work. I was hoping my mind would focus and I would think clearly. I carried on with my work and kept my home life separate.

Separation and Divorce

Now the police have been in contact with me and said that Gurjit will be going to court and will not be allowed within a certain distance of the house, myself or the children. Gurjit has been charged and sentenced to three months in prison. It has been made public knowledge because it appeared in the newspapers. I am in shock and not knowing what to do and what to say to anyone. Family and friends were all shocked and would say to me that I looked happy all the time and was always smiling.

Only my neighbours knew about some of the abuse and would see him drunk in the streets coming home. What was I supposed to do? I had been in an arranged marriage at an early age when I was naive. I still went to work and my Dad helped with looking after the children.

The story about me didn't take long to spread around because I got looks from people that I didn't know at work.

I could have done without it but I guess it is gossip for others to talk about. Also at home I am getting his side of the family hounding me and banging on my door, but I pretend that I'm not home and stay upstairs. They did notice someone in the house, sometimes, as they must have seen the curtain move. They even had the cheek to go to the house across the road asking them to talk with me; but they did not get involved. They waited a long time before they decided to leave.

Even from prison Gurjit had been sending me visiting passes. He also got someone else to write me a letter apologising and asking if I would visit him. He also told me how he loved me and saying that I would not be able to cope or live without him. I couldn't believe it, after what he put me through, he still thought he did nothing wrong.

After his release from prison, he went to stay with his sister Daljit and was now communicating with me through his relatives.

A relative of his had told me that he would take responsibility for him, if I would take him back and that nothing like that would happen to me again.

Gurjit also arranged to have a meeting with myself, my brothers and his uncles at Larry's house; as I would feel comfortable there. As I talked and he talked he confessed that he did nothing wrong and that all marriages had their ups and downs and that ours was no different. I was not having any of it although inside myself I was shaking, just by being in the same room as him; but I had to compose myself.

Of our three children, Michael and Sarah went to secondary school and Thomas went to junior school. Gurjit would appear outside their schools on different days. Sarah didn't like it and would try to avoid him and she would tell me about it. On another occasion when he did speak with Sarah he would ask what I was up to. When he saw Michael it was different because he would take him to the shop to buy sweets hoping to get information from him. Another time he appeared at Thomas' school. I had found out from the teachers that Gurjit was asking them where Thomas was. I was getting concerned about the children's safety that I started to pick them up from school in the car.

Sometimes I even saw Gurjit outside the school. Once, I even stopped the car next to him and told him not to come to their school as they are becoming unsettled. He looked straight at me and said that I had changed; I said that I wasn't scared of him anymore and that there is nothing he can do to me. Then I drove off.

I'm still doing shift work and my Dad comes to my house and stays with the children. Once, when I was at work, a call is passed to me asking me to come home because the police were there. All thoughts were going through my head thinking "Are my children OK?" What could have happened? It took me fifteen minutes to get home and when I got there the police had already left.

I saw blood on the door and a smashed door window panel. As soon as I got in the house my children hugged me; my dad was terrified.

What happened was, Gurjit came to the house and no one opened the door to him so he smashed the glass panel and unlocked the door to gain entry. By then Michael and Sarah had run upstairs and locked the bedroom door. Gurjit went upstairs telling them to open the door my dad had run across the road for help asking the neighbours to phone the police. In the bedroom the kids managed to push the bed in front of the door and Sarah also rang the police as I had a telephone in that room. As soon as the police arrived they arrested Gurjit and after questioning they released him because he broke into his own house. Thomas was staying with my Mum at the time.

I have taken some holiday time off work because I had so much to sort out. I got some legal advice and took out a court order to keep Gurjit away from the house and school.

I was also given full custody of our children and Gurjit was given visits, one day a week with supervision. He didn't even visit the children once on those terms.

I decided to go for a divorce and took legal advice and I now needed a solicitor. I've had half an hour of free consultation telling me what to expect. I know this is what I want for me and my children; it's been a long time but now we are going to be free. As I was working I couldn't get legal aid, so I had to pay in full. I asked if it would be ok to pay instalments as it was going to cost me thousands.

At home I've packed all of Gurjit's clothing and put them in a couple of large suitcases, then I called a taxi and I told the driver that these suitcases were to be drop off at his sister's house and I gave the address. I told the driver that they are expecting them and I will pay up front. The taxi man was surprised that I wasn't travelling with the luggage.

I got to hear what happened when the taxi arrived at the address where Gurjit was staying. Daljit refused to accept the suitcases, however, the taxi driver said that I had already paid him and left them outside her house.

I am so excited because it's all happening and I want to redecorate the house. I loved wallpapering and putting my own touch on the place. At the moment it was all dreams, but they were my dreams. I also needed money to pay the solicitors fees and money to buy his share of the house. My dad was very supportive and helped me financially.

I had some gold from my wedding that I had decided to sell, that raised more money to buy his share of the house. I also said to the solicitor's that we had a house in India and I would sign all rights over to Gurjit. Our house was now my home with my children.

I Am Broken

I am finally divorced now and have come to the end of this chapter of my life. What I did to celebrate was get a tattoo on my right arm, it was a band of roses and a little heart and it meant a lot to me as I saw it as victory; I still see it as that to this day. I was also the first in our family to get a tattoo. It was painful and as I worked with food I had to keep it bandaged over.

Life was still challenging as I always had my children on my mind when I was at work. I would imagine their whereabouts, knowing that they were at school and when they would be on their lunch break.

Once I had a call come to my work and as it came to me I was told that the school had rang. They said that a man called them and advised that Michael was not coming back to school for the afternoon. My first thoughts were that Gurjit has something to do with it.

I asked for time away from work and got home as quick as I could. Michael and his friend were surprised to see me at home. I asked them what they were doing at home and not at school. Michael said that they came home to get his games kit and were going back to school. I even offered to drop them off at school. After listening to their lies I told them that the school had rang my work and said that a man had rang.

I told Michael this was no joking matter and how worried I was. I also found out that it wasn't the first time he was truanting from school. Michael confessed that when he and his friend saw my car leaving for work that's when they would come back into the house.

My contract with work was coming to an end and I was already struggling with my health. I constantly had pain in my back; the doctors had been sending me for physiotherapy for weeks. I was also coping with family life as I was being a mum and a dad to my children now.

I had spoken with my employers, who were very supportive; I decided that I was not going to have another six months contract. My work chapter had come to an end after working in all the different departments for five years.

I've decided to give the house a makeover and wanted to put our touch to make it homely. I started by having double glazed windows put in, although I would have preferred brown frames; I couldn't afford them. Instead I had white. As I loved doing the decorating; I am doing the children's bedrooms. Michael and Thomas shared a bedroom and now we were going to put two beds in the room, I decorated the room with their choices of design and Sarah had a room decorated to her choosing.

I loved seeing the kids laughing and being happy. In my mind I had a design of seeing our house with a conservatory and a bigger kitchen with a downstairs toilet room. I would talk to the kids about my dreams and they would ask me "Mum when is it going to happen?

I would say "one day it's going to happen and I'm not going to stop hoping. At the moment we are going to make do with what we have." The carpet was next to being replaced and I shopped for the remnants which were the room sizes and value for money. I didn't have enough money to buy new sofas so I would put a little money aside to save as I had seen twin sofas that I liked. The out of date kitchen had the doors changed which gave it a modern new look. Our house was now a home.

I was broken inside and needed a makeover. The pain in my back was persisted and I kept taking pain killers, my past would come to the front and I didn't know how to deal with it. My doctor suggested that counselling would be good. After waiting for an appointment I was seen, on a weekly basis, for an hour at a time and I openly shared my life with the counsellor. I was told that I had been mowed down like a road roller that was used to put tarmac in the road and now I had to rebuild my life.

I stayed in touch with a couple of work colleagues; Baljinder and Dave.

It was months later that I heard that Dave had separated from his wife and was going through a divorce. He bought himself a three bedroom house which was in need of decorating and as we were friends, my heart went out to him. I would ask Dave to come over to our house after work and have a cooked meal. He was struggling financially and needed to borrow five hundred pounds; he was going to get a bank loan.

In my heart, I wanted to lend him the money that I had saved but I was uncertain because of past money issues. I thought about it for a few days before going to visit Dave to offer him the money. He hadn't asked and he was so surprised that he said "you could blow me down with a feather," it meant so much to him. He said that he would pay me back the following month.

I continued to have counselling and each time more hurt and upset would come to the surface. I was told that I was like a picture without a frame. I was lost and vulnerable, not knowing where to turn. A guy from my previous workplace started to show an interest in me which I followed and started dating. We had been dating a while when I realised it was not what I wanted. He didn't like the response so I had to get the police involved.

I didn't know what was happening to me, I was struggling with life; feeling depressed and even tried alcohol but it made me sick. I also tried smoking to help me feel better; this was in my bedroom with the door closed and the window open. My son and daughter would knock on the bedroom door telling me that they could smell burning and would ask if I was OK, "I'm fine" I would say, while all the time the room was spinning; but that didn't help me either.

As time went by being a home mum, I didn't have a social life with friends and my family could not understand the stress I was suffering. I had struggled with the opening of my heart and would put on a front.

My kids were in full time education and with the time I had during the day I would help Dave decorate his house whilst he was at work. He thought wallpapering was easy until he had a go and couldn't get it to line up straight; it was best that he left it to me. Dave kept his word and paid me back the money that I had loaned to him.

My children were familiar with Dave and he invited us all around for a meal as a thank you. Although he cooked and followed a recipe, it did look good but it didn't agree with our stomachs. At our home Dave would help us with electrics and other DIY jobs, I also told my dad who Dave was; he also would help my dad with his DIY. My mum would ask me if we were a couple and I told her that we were friends.

I was doing some gardening and on one occasion I had been cutting the lawn using an extension lead to get the lawnmower to the top of the garden. I pulled it a little too far and it had stopped working. I thought it was the wiring that had come out so I unplugged the lawnmower and took the extension lead into the laundry area and I started to unscrew the plug. Now the wiring was exposed and two of the wires touched my hand and I was getting electric shocks. On my left was the fridge and for some reason I had felt in my heart not to put my hand on the fridge and I kept about ten inches away, before realising that I hadn't switched off the other side of the extension lead at the main socket.

My hand was left with tiny holes and when Dave came over to our house after work he was asking me what I had done to my hand. As I started telling him what had happened I was laughing and said that it was nothing new to me as I am always doing things like this and forgetting which wiring goes where. The look on Dave's face was serious and I noticed his eyes had filled with tears as he said "I could have lost you today," I couldn't understand why though. He explained that I could have been electrocuted if I had touched the fridge. I explained that I felt in my heart not too and I didn't. He then got hold of the extension lead and put it straight in the dustbin and said he is going to get me a new one with a protective circuit breaker and asked me not to do anything again involving electricity and to always ask him to do it as he was an electrician.

We would both go shopping together and when Dave came around to pick me up I was always vacuuming downstairs and the stairs before I left the house. Dave would always say that my house was always clean, it's because I had got used to cleaning every day before leaving the house. Sometimes I would be doing my prayers when Dave came to the house and he would help by doing the vacuuming. He would see me praying and ask why I was using a beaded necklace to pray with. I was seeking God as I was broken and needed healing in my soul. In my prayer time I saw a vision of a man who would be coming into my life. When I saw this vision I opened my eyes and said to God "that man is my friend Dave and I don't fancy him." I didn't tell him at the time.

I was having pains in my body and went to see a lady who did massages at her home. She also told me that she can see a man who is slim, tall with glasses and has a moustache who is going to come into my life and look after me because no one else did. She had never met Dave and I said to her "he is already in my life." She was describing Dave. It confirmed to me what I had seen; she also told me that she was a Christian. I didn't understand it, how can she be a Christian when she is an Indian?

A year has passed since Dave had been living in his home and he has come over to go shopping together. Over a cup of tea, Dave said that he didn't want to make the mistake of meeting someone else then knowing he would miss the chance of being with me. He knew how badly I had been hurt in the past. In my thoughts I knew he was not going to meet anyone else and at the same time I couldn't see myself with him. So I came out with it and told him what I had seen in my prayers and what the massage lady had spoken of. Dave was saying that he would never hurt me and that he would wait for me as long as it took. He said he would 'wrap me in cotton wool.' I made an appointment with the massage lady and I took Dave along with me. We arrived at her house and as soon as she opened her front door she said "this is the man I saw." We stayed for tea and chatted; she had never seen Dave before and was surprised. At home I spoke with my children and asked them how they would feel if I decided to get married to Dave in the future? "Mum, we want to see you happy" was their reply. In my heart I wanted the children's happiness and that they would be fine with Dave.

Engagement and Marriage

We decided to go and visit my parents and while we were there Dave asked my Dad if he could have my hand in marriage. My Dad looked straight at him and said "make sure you never lay a hand on her" then my Mum told him to put my hand in Dave's. As my Dad put my hand in Dave's hand he gave us his blessing. Inside myself I was hesitant.

Dave wanted the day we got engaged to be special so he spoke about taking me in a hot air balloon. In my heart I didn't feel ready to get married again as I was haunted by my past and as Dave was my best friend; I didn't want to hurt him. So every time Dave checked if the weather was ok for flying I would be praying that it would be cancelled. On three occasions it was cancelled and a year had passed. During that year a cousin was having problems with her teenage daughter and I said it would be ok if she wanted to stay with us for a while.

We talked about life and she said some things. I remember saying that you never forget things that happen when you are a kid. I told her what happened when I was a kid. I didn't think anything of it until it came out. She became a handful and after many weeks she went back home. What I had said to her spread like gossip.

My Dad got to hear about it and when I went to see my Dad he asked me if it was true. I said it was and he said to me I know you are telling the truth because you do not lie. I was accused of trying to break the family. The abuser started making threats towards my Dad and making him feel uncomfortable. When I heard of this I told my Dad not to worry. I got the number of the abuser, I rang him up and I told him "leave my Dad alone and I will say it never happened."

My Dad never got bothered again. I felt like I was reliving my past and I had no escape. My Dad was getting sick more often now; I would bury my feelings and pain to help him.

I would take him to his appointments and support him in any way I could. One day my Dad took me to the jewellery shop and bought me a gold necklace; it's the only way he showed his love. My Mum knew I had been saving for a new sofa so she was offering me seven hundred pounds towards it. I said "Mum if you are giving me the money because I have been looking after Dad then I don't want it." When I told her that; I didn't get the money. The following week she gave the money to my daughter Sarah and told her to use the money towards her driving lessons when she was going to have them. I stayed silent.

Dad wasn't getting any better and as it was his seventieth birthday, I thought it would be nice to surprise him with a birthday cake. It was the first birthday cake my Dad ever had; the smile on his face when he saw it said it all. He gave me, Dave and the children five pounds each to spend. That was a day I will always remember.

While I was looking after my Dad my friend Baljinder would ring me every couple of days asking for a lift to her mum's house as her mum was ill. I didn't want to say no because I did not know how to. I would pick her up and drive for twenty minutes to her mum's and then another twenty minutes to my Dad's house. I had helped her for many months and I felt I was being used as a taxi; but I continued to give her lifts until her mother passed away. After that I had no more contact with her.

The hospital had said it would be better for my Dad to be in a care home as there was nothing more the hospital could do as he had been ill for three years.

It was a Friday afternoon when Ricky and I went to visit him in hospital. Dad looked so frail and I remember washing his glasses as Ricky cut his nails before putting him in bed; then I kissed his forehead and said goodbye. It was the last time I would see my Dad alive.

That evening he was moved to a care home and passed away in the early hours of Sunday morning. It was Ricky's wife that rang me on Sunday and told me that Dad had passed away. I was upset that I was the last to hear about it.

Arrangements were made for his funeral and while I was at my Dad's house the abuser was also there in the front room; I was in the living room. I knew it was the right time so I stood up, my legs were shaking and I went to the front room and confronted him. I said "My Dad is dead and now I want an apology from you." He looked straight to my face and told me that I wasn't getting one. I stood still and said "if I don't get one tomorrow you just wait and see."

Next day we are at Mum's house again and I am in the kitchen cooking when Mum calls me into the downstairs bedroom. When I entered the room the abuser is there with her and wants to apologise. I looked straight at him and he said "I apologise" I said "apologise then" so he said "I am sorry," I replied "go in peace." Now the little girl in me can rest.

I continued to pray and read my bible. As I prayed to the gods I saw in a vision that when we were to be in a hot air balloon getting engaged; I saw signs in the sky from the gods. When the day came, we went to the town where we were going to have our hot air balloon experience. I was so excited that I was to see a sign in the sky when I got engaged.

We are back on the ground after the experience and it's seven in the evening, we told the host that we have just become engaged so he gave us some champagne and a certificate to commemorate our balloon flight. I was pleased that I had received my Father's blessing before he passed away and missed him greatly.

All the time I kept looking up towards the sky and Dave asked me what I was looking at. As we were walking back towards the car, he was holding my hand and I still kept looking back and up towards the sky, but I saw nothing; nothing at all. I was asking myself "how can this be." We walked out of the park and as we were passing a church the church bells started to ring and a choir started to sing. I walked up to the church steps and listened, how can this be? I looked at my watch and the time was seven fifty. The sound was beautiful and angelic; I still remember it to this day. I didn't understand why the church bells rang because I was waiting for a sign from the gods and they don't go to the church.

When we got home we celebrated with the children and enjoyed an engagement cake. We all then went to Disneyland Paris. The children had a great time and they chose a cuddly toy each, I had a Minnie mouse which was three feet tall. Dave said that I needed to have Mickey mouse as well. I still have them to this day; sitting on top of our wardrobe. They are now a collection of many Disney cuddly toys that have accumulated over time.

I continued to pray in my prayer closet each morning and read my little red bible, I'm always asking for help with my life, not knowing how I can keep living with the way my health was. I told the gods that I wanted to live my life up until my youngest child Thomas became eighteen. Then I would know that I have done my duty as a mother and after that, if I was to die, I knew that they were adults. I had shared this with Dave before I decided to get engaged.

Dave suggested that I try acupuncture with herbal medicine. So we arranged an appointment with a local doctor and when I had my first treatment I felt so emotional. When it had finished I came out with a smile and didn't understand why we both were laughing. Dave took care of the payments and I continued having treatment and taking herbal medicine.

Over time it stopped having the effect. I was emotional and unstable; unable to cope with life. I would be tired throughout the day, the pain in my back was unbearable, I would even lie on the floor to give my back a stretch and when it came to getting up I would struggle immensely. My mind would flood with suicidal thoughts and I would cry "no, not now! My children are young and I have to think about living." I would cry to the gods asking them to help me, help me! Is anyone going to help me? I was feeling a force that wanted me to commit suicide by hanging myself in the garage.

I stopped myself from being pushed through the kitchen door by stretching my arms out. I calmed down after a while and then Dave came home. I was surprised to see him. Dave was supposed to be at work when he said he felt in his heart that he needed to come home. He asked his employer for a couple of hours off. Dave stayed with me and calmed me down and as I was resting he said he had to get back to work and I said I would be ok. I must have fallen asleep and I started to dream that I was with my three children in a dug out pit which was the size of a double coffin. Looking out of the pit I saw there was green grass on the other side of the road; it was a large green area and it was beautiful. I then said to my children that I was going to help them out and they were to run across to the other side and stay there. As I helped them out one by one, I saw them playing together and was filled with joy. I felt peace as I watched. I felt ok where I was until I decided that I had to get out and run so I could be with them. As I got out and ran to be with my children a puff of darkness left and I woke up. Soon my children would be coming home from school and I was to get their dinner ready.

Dave would be coming round at seven in the evening and we would have our meal together; we talked about living as a family. I asked my children how they felt about Dave moving in with us. Our house was a three bedroom semi-detached and Dave's house had two bedrooms, so it made sense for Dave to move in and live with us; rather than move into his house.

I didn't want to sell our house to by another as I had memories of my children growing up in this house.

Dave would stay with us a few nights in the week to begin with. It wasn't long before the benefits agent came round asking me if he had moved in permanently as they had received a complaint. I didn't have any enemies but I knew it was one of the neighbours living nearby. They had problems with their daughter-in-law and we didn't turn our backs on her when she cried for help; we opened our door to her without getting involved and they didn't like it. A few weeks later another complaint was made about me it was given to the same officer that received the first complaint and he knew my situation, but he still had to investigate the matter and I was still doing nothing wrong.

While we were having work done on the driveway we asked the other neighbour if we could park our car in their drive, they said yes. The car was parked in their drive over night and when I went to it in the morning the back window was smashed and a brick was found in the car. We got the police involved but no finger prints would be found on a rock. We got the screen replaced and I went round with a brush and swept all the glass the best I could. I asked the neighbours if they saw anyone or heard any noise but they said they didn't.

I continued to have counselling once a week, although the improvements were small; I was moving forward. My emotions were like a roller coaster. I was constantly taking tablets for the pain in my back and I was sent to have more physiotherapy; this time it was a different therapist. As she was working down my spine she stopped and said that I should go back to my general practitioner and ask for a MRI scan to be done. She said that it felt that my back was not right and she was going to stop the treatment. A few days later I had got an appointment with my doctor's and told him what the physiotherapist had said so he referred me to the hospital for a MRI scan. I had to wait for three months before I was seen and then another two weeks before I got the results. All of a sudden I got a phone call from a surgeon from the hospital giving me an appointment to attend. As I attended I was seen by a spinal surgeon who asked me how I had got the spinal injuries. I told him that I had injured myself at work doing some heavy lifting. He also asked how long ago it happened, I thought it was about four to five years but he said the injuries are about seven years old. When I thought properly about it he was right.

He also asked me how I had managed to get on with my life the way I was. I told him that it was with great difficulty because I had three children to look after and I wasn't going to give up on them or myself, so I kept on going. The injuries had escalated and I had a crushed disc, drained out disc, crushed bone and a lopsided disc. The doctor suggested that the crushed disc needed to be removed as it was pressing on the nerves and was causing sciatica. Within two days of seeing the doctor at the hospital I was given an emergency appointment to have surgery; I was going to have an operation. Finally it was a relief to know what had been causing me to be ill so much.

All went well with the operation; I had to stay in hospital until I was able to walk up a flight of stairs. It was four days later when the physiotherapist came and asked me if I would like to try and walk. There were two nurses with me and it felt as if I was climbing a mountain. However, I managed to walk up and down the stairs before they walked me back to my room. I felt so exhausted that when I came back to my bed I collapsed. I came round a few hours later and told the nurse what happened. One nurse said she thought I was asleep when she came to see me. The doctor came and requested a blood test which showed that my blood count was low and I needed to have a blood transfusion.

I would be staying for another couple of days in hospital. During this time Dave would take care of my children, making them meals and also visiting me; as well as going to work.

It is time for me to come home and Dave is picking me up. I even felt all the road bumps coming home even though Dave drove slowly. I have been given two crutches to get around on and was given the medication I needed to help me recover. It's the start of another journey. The pain was excruciating and I need to rest a lot, which I found difficult as I was always on the go looking after the family. Now the family was looking after me. I would try and come down the stairs, when I got to the kitchen all I wanted to do was clean. It wasn't to my usual standard which made me feel more sick. I felt as if I had let the family down by not cooking and cleaning. I would be overwhelmed by guilt and would keep apologising because they were looking after me; but I would be better soon and then I could carry on looking after them.

Dave kept reassuring me that everything was ok and that the house was clean and tidy. In my eyes it wasn't and I couldn't get my head around it. After four weeks I was taking more steps and continued with physiotherapy even though I was still getting pain in my spine. I have been given a follow up appointment to have X-rays and when I saw the doctor to talk about them he had said that there is nothing more we can do. He told me to get on with my life the best I can and then slammed my file shut.

I told him that I still have hope and left the room. I found the doctor to be blunt with no compassion. I knew that I had hope because my little bible told me in 1 Corinthians 13:13 *'Now abideth faith, hope and love, these three; but the greatest of these is love.'*

I am getting along a lot better now, as long as I don't overdo things; I used to be like a tornado getting everything done. I'm doing the cooking but sharing the housework with the children, I have taught them all to iron their own clothes and how to cook; also to hang out the washed laundry. My children are a credit and a blessing to me.

It has been three years since Dave and I got engaged so I asked Dave "Shall we get married?" He was so happy when I came out with it because he had asked me so many times. I felt it was time. We decided that he would sell his house so we could live together as a family.

A tragedy happened, a close family relative had committed suicide and when I heard about it I went round their house. In my heart I felt I was going to meet someone there. I had been there for about an hour or so when the doorbell rang. I felt in my heart that I was going to meet that person, so I got up and went into the hall to see who had arrived. I recognised the lady from my childhood and when I saw her I said her name; I knew that she had changed her religion. She asked me who I was "I'm Baljit" I said. When she heard my name she took me by the hand and we went into the study room and closed the door. "What is it?" I asked, she told me that I was to choose which side of the fence I was going to be on. I didn't understand what she was saying. She then said that I was worshipping both idols and Jesus. I said that I was as they are all gods and that there was no difference. She told me that this wasn't true and that I had to choose right now who I was going to follow. I said alright I will choose Jesus. So she asked me to repeat a prayer after her and then she told me that I had become a Christian. However, I didn't feel any different so we exchanged telephone numbers and said we would stay in touch. When I got home I continued to pray and worship idols. I continued with my routine and when Bella rang me and asked how I was getting on with my life, I said that I was praying as I always did. As she explained about the bible to me, I understood some of it and that I should stop praying the way I was and I should clean the prayer closet out. I still didn't understand why but I did because I was a Christian.

Bella also mentioned that there was a church, in my town that was recommended by her Pastor and that I should go there. I didn't have a clue where it was and I'm thinking "no way am I going to a church on my own." The only time that I ever went to a church was at harvest time with my school; even then I didn't understand what was going on. I told Dave about it, he was a Christian but he wasn't a practising Christian who went to church.

Every time I spoke with Bella she would mention this church but I still had no idea of where it was because, as I found out, they had moved to a different location due to renovating. I continued to read the bible and one morning as Dave and I were having our breakfast in the conservatory, I was about to put my anti-depression tablet in my mouth when I heard a voice in my heart telling me not to take the tablet. I paused and told Dave what I had heard and didn't take the medication. I stopped them completely and for the first few days it felt like 'cold turkey.' After that I was fine with no depression. Wow! I thought this God called Jesus is good.

Arrangements are being made for our wedding and we decided it was going to be a close family occasion. We got some handmade wedding invitations and balloons from eBay. It was going to be a registry office marriage. It turned out to be a bright sunny day; I wore a blue sari and a gold necklace which was a gift from my brother Ricky. My shoes were a gift from sister Manpreet and my Mum gave the gift of paying the food bill. Dave wore a blue suit. Sarah bought us Mickey and Minnie limited edition wedding bears. Michael and Thomas bought us engraved champagne glasses and Michael's friend made the wedding cake.

My Mum did not attend as she wasn't well so we all went round to her house after the wedding and had photographs taken with her. The celebration continued in the evening at the restaurant and everyone had a great time.

Later on in the night we cut the strings off the heart shaped balloons and watched them go up into the sky. A few weeks later we were all excited and ready to go on a three week family holiday to Florida, where we rented a villa and hired a car to travel around in. We all had an amazing time going around all the theme parks and shopping malls.

Another joyous occasion was seeing our daughter Sarah graduate from university with two award ceremonies. We were so proud of her achievement that she was the only one in her year to receive an award for her dissertation. After we had the photographs taken we went for a meal, then I put on Sarah's graduation gown and hat and had my picture taken with Dave. That was another dream that had come true as I have never been to university. Sarah also passed her driving test and we surprised her with a car of her choice.

Seeking God

Since becoming a Christian this was going to be my first visit to a church in June 2009. Bella has come over to stay with us for a couple of days. She had spoken about this church for many years but I never had the courage to go and see for myself. We have decided to go together as it will also be Bella's first visit at this church.

It is a Sunday morning and we are getting ready to go to church. I am feeling nervous because I am not sure what to expect. When we arrived at the church, which is called All Nations, we were greeted by the Pastor known as Steve Uppal; he was welcoming.

Bella introduced herself and told the Pastor that this church had been recommended by another Pastor from London. She said that she was visiting from London and then introduced me. The church was nothing like I thought it would be. There were no candles, pulpits or vicars. It had a stage and lots of chairs that were in rows.

We went and sat in the second row. A lady walked passed us on the front row and she smiled at me, I couldn't understand why! I didn't know her; although I felt at ease. Later I found out that she was Esther the Pastor's wife.

 All of a sudden I burst out crying. Bella turned to me and she asked "What's wrong? Are you OK? She has wrapped her arms around me; I'm crying more and more and that's when I said "I'm home, I'm home." I described it as 'loving arms wrapped around me, like a Father loves his child.' The embrace was so powerful, loving, warm and secure.

The next visit to the church was going to be in a hall in the city centre, which was holding a conference in July 2009. Now I didn't know what a conference was or what was going to happen there, so Dave and I are going to go. The meeting was starting at seven in the evening and doors were to open at six. The hall seated around five hundred people and when everyone was seated it was full.

Pastor Steve announced a guest speaker, who was an Evangelist; he was doing a United Kingdom tour. He was talking about God, from darkness to light, the divine healer at work. We all stood up singing praises to God when all of a sudden my arms went up into the air. I had not been able to raise my arms due to my spinal injury.

I felt warmth in my body and I'm streaming with tears, the Evangelist was speaking the word from the Bible declaring healing for the sick. He said aloud that anyone with thyroid problems along with names of other sicknesses "Be Healed!" I had thyroid problems and as he spoke those words my thyroids melted away like ice cubes. Then he tells everyone to do something that they couldn't do before. I looked to my husband and said "I'm going to jump." I lifted my feet and jumped nearly falling on the man behind me as I lost my balance. When the preaching was done the evangelist asked that anyone who received healing in their body to come to the front and share what they received from God. Many people shared how God touched them and were healed. I also went to the front and said that I've been healed and how I couldn't jump. The guy at the front was confused when he looked at me and asked "What do you mean you couldn't jump?" I did explain and I was asked onto the platform to share my testimony as to what took place.

 I told the evangelist that I had spinal injuries which stopped me from lifting both my feet together. Also I had thyroid problems which had just melted away. He asked if I would jump to testify to everyone. I said Yes I would! The band started to sing 'Oh, happy day, happy day, I'll never be the same, forever I am changed" Hallelujah!

I am ready to see if I can still jump - I paused. Then I jumped and jumped again with my arms in the air. I saw the crowd jumping with me and praising God for my mighty miracle. Hallelujah! My husband was weeping and the lady next to him asked him if he knew me? He replied yes! She's my wife and she was not able to do that!

Having being overwhelmed with joy, I had to get my head round to what had happened; I was able to run and jump. When we came home I shared with the children what had happened, it was a lot for them to take in. We were emotional and happy with joy that I had received a miracle, we had heard of miracles happening and now I had one.

A couple of weeks later it was announced at the church that a baptismal service was going to take place, I asked about what it meant. It was for the people who have accepted Jesus Christ as their Lord and Saviour. It involved being committed to Jesus and being briefly put under water and lifted up again; it was called being born again.

After asking about it, I was interested so I put my name down to be baptised. I shared with the family that I was getting baptised, my children also said that they wanted to get baptised. Our children had accepted Jesus Christ as their Lord and Saviour. I had died to self and had risen in Christ, with my children, we all got baptised on the same day in October 2009. Dave got baptised a few months later when he was ready in his heart and got born again.

I was healed physically and mentally, although I would remember the past torments and grief that I had been through and how it had affected my children. That would make me feel unsettled as if I was being plagued by past memories. Each time when the thoughts came back it was as if the past tried to get into my present; to stop me from moving forward towards my future.

I was an anxious person and I would go to the church on Sunday's with Dave and ask for prayers. I would put on a smile as if nothing was going on but inside I was broken. I didn't know how to release the bottled up emotions that were built up inside.

I went to my Mum's and Ricky's wife was there and I told them how I got healed and I jumped to show them. Ricky's wife was surprised although I didn't see any sign of excitement from my Mum; this left me feeling low. It felt as if anything I did didn't make her happy.

At our church Pastor Steve asked me if I would be willing to share my testimony at a television station. I was so excited and I said Yes! There were many of us who would be sharing testimonies including my husband; who had been healed from a heart condition. In the following days we went to the UCB (United Christian Broadcasters) studio where the testimonies were recorded. The testimonies are on YouTube named My Story Baljit and My Story Dave.

On another occasion Pastor Steve asked me if I would share my testimony during an event that the Church was holding in Queen Square Wolverhampton; I said that I would.

Whilst we were there I handed out 'Guess Who' booklets to the public. These booklets described who we were in Christ and what Jesus did for us at the Cross. All the while I was getting more and more nervous because I knew I would be speaking in public for the first time. Pastor Steve got my attention and called me over to speak. I looked around for Dave hoping he would stand with me but he was busy and I couldn't catch his eye.

I was given the microphone and there was a silent pause before I started to share my testimony. When my testimony was finished, I then spoke the words "it doesn't matter where you have been, or what you have done, come home" the people in the square went silent and gazed at me in awe. After a pause the square erupted in thunderous applause.

Dave and I loved doing our own home DIY and as the back of our garden was so uneven we decided to build a decking. Dave ordered all the parts and together it took us six months to put it together. We started the work in winter so it would be ready for the summer; that's when we varnished the boards and railings. When we finished it was so big that we laughed that a helicopter might come and land on it.

A few days later we went shopping to the Saddlers centre in Walsall hoping to get some bargains; we shopped around and soon got peckish so we got a pasty each to eat. As we were walking through the main shopping mall, we saw two men who were arguing with each other very loudly. We walked passed them and decided to sit in the bus shelter and eat our pasty. The two guys came into the bus shelter on the other side and continued with their arguing.

I looked over at them and all of a sudden I gave my pasty to Dave to hold and I got up and walked over to them and stood still. The two guys went quiet when I said, with my hands in my pocket; "may I intervene?"

One guy nodded his head in a yes. I then said "You are both Gods children and he loves you both." One of the guys kissed my hand and agreed, the other guy just stared at me as I walked back to Dave, sat down and carried on eating my pasty and I said "did that just happen?" Soon the bus shelter filled with people and we left.

We bought a hammock that I had always wanted and a table with four chairs. We also bought a parasol to keep off the sun. We were so proud that we did the work ourselves and pleased with the way it turned out, our home was turning into an even lovelier home.

Everything Dave and I did we did together.

One sunny afternoon, as I was sitting on the hammock, I was in a conversation with God and I wrote this poem:

Amazing Grace Touched
Me and You alone
In the shadows
Breeze in the meadows
On a day like this
Smile upon my face
My heart trembles
Deep in thought
Enjoying my time with you, amazing!
I find it hard to relax
I smile, I'm smitten
What is going on? I laugh.

We also planned to get the house extended by having an extra bedroom, a toilet room downstairs and a bigger kitchen. We decided to have the shell of the extension built so that we would get the inside built and decorated ourselves. Dave had some money from the sale of his house which paid towards the extension; gold prices were also very high so I sold my gold. I got a good price and put the money towards the furnishings.

The building and plasterer's mess was so overwhelming that I would clean every evening; ready for the builders to start again the next day. I would watch and see our dreams coming together and I imagined a top of the range kitchen. The young adults would finally be getting a room to themselves. Sometimes during the day I would go to my Mums and help her, I would see if she needed any shopping and I would go and buy it.

One day she wanted some Asian food so I went to buy it and as I was driving back to Mums, a car reversed out of their driveway and smashed into the driver's side sending my car off the road. I felt as if I was seeing stars. After a while I managed to get out of the car and I went to see if the driver of the other car was OK. When she saw me, she got out of her car and said she was sorry and that it was her fault and we exchanged details. I managed to drive the car back to my mums and delivered her food.

I acted normal until she had finished eating her meal, then I told her about the accident. She felt guilty because she asked me to go to the shops. I told Mum that it could have happened at any time and not to be upset, I then drove the car back home. The insurance took care of the situation and they said that the car was a write off and had it scrapped; that was my favourite car.

I started looking on the internet for a replacement. I had prayed asking Jesus to help me choose another car. Even though I had always bought a Vauxhall, the car I felt was the right one was a Ford Focus. The specification looked good and the pictures were also good so I asked Dave to have a look. As it was a Friday Dave said that it would be Monday before we get to look at the vehicle and that it might get sold before then. I had such peace in my heart that we bought it online. The car was delivered to our home the following week, it was immaculate. We still have the same car today.

The house looked in such a mess because of the work and the original windows looked old. As we were having new windows on the extension, Dave suggested that we change the windows on the rest of the house. I was surprised when Dave said that he remembered I always wanted brown window frames, now we can have them.

We got a loan as we added the extras on. Dave was an engineer and I was the decorator so all the inside work was going to be done by ourselves. It took three months for the builders to complete their work and as the builders were tidying up and loading their vans, I stepped on the edge of a board at an angle and tripped. I didn't think much of it at the time but I do remember that the builders work finished in September 2011. I had spent a lot of time cleaning and it was now time to prepare the evening meal. As I am cooking I'm feeling pain in my lower back, I remember saying to my husband that after dinner I am going to have an early night; I was feeling tired.

My Hope in God

It has gone eight in the evening and I am feeling cramp in my left thigh which was making me unable to sleep; I never thought of it as anything wrong. As I sat on the bed with my legs down I was leaning on the headboard. The cramp was getting so annoying that I took a pillow and the quilt and lied down on the floor.

It is still not any better; I'm in so much pain and I couldn't understand how cramp could be so painful. It was almost midnight before I got into bed and fell asleep. I woke up the next morning and moved the quilt off me, ready to get out of bed to start another day. As I started to get out of bed I fell on the floor.

My God! My God! What's happened to me? I cannot move my left leg and my left foot is crippled. I am in shock and I am crying. I can't get my head round this, I said aloud "Someone help me, help me!" My husband Dave had already gone to work.

Michael, Sarah and Thomas came into my bedroom "What's happened Mum? Are you OK?" They helped me get up onto the bed. The horror of shock on their faces; I had to be strong. They helped me around the bedroom and then to the top of the stairs where I came down the stairs on my bottom and sat on a chair. The pain was indescribable.

I rang the Doctors surgery and told the receptionist what had happened and requested a home visit. When the Doctor arrived I told him what had happened and that I was in so much pain and crying; I've been prescribed Diazepam and Co-codamol.

A week has passed taking the medicine; I'm not feeling any better, so I've requested another home visit from the surgery. This time it was a different Doctor and I went through explaining it all again and about the medicine I was taking. Even he could see the state that I was in and said that I should come off the diazepam.

Another week has passed and I'm still not any better, so I requested another visit from the surgery. This doctor said to take the tablets as needed, now I'm so confused, that I didn't take the tablets.

The pain is so unbearable, that now I've been prescribed Tramadol. On taking one of these tablets, it has knocked me senseless; I don't remember laying down and not getting up or knowing my whereabouts. I am not taking another one of these tablets, so I had them returned to the chemist.

In the mornings I would do my prayers and Michael would bring me breakfast and a cup of tea. I would be thinking of what I can do today as I wasn't going anywhere crippled. I felt as if I was just existing and not living. Each morning Michael would bring me breakfast, one time he surprised me with a McDonald's breakfast burger. I would have thoughts of me jumping for joy in praise, singing 'Oh Happy Day' to the Lord.

Each morning again I would pray and ask the Lord to help me, I would get dressed to feel good and then rest again. I realised how we can lose track of who we are as individuals as we put our family first. Whatever is left we use to think of ourselves.

I thank the Lord God Almighty who has us in the palm of his hands. He brings to us complete healing and restoration. Life is to be enjoyed as a blessing from God.

A few weeks have passed and I spent most of my time upstairs as I was struggling to hobble on my right leg. I would come downstairs, step by step, sitting on my bottom. After a while I would struggle to get back upstairs as we only had one bathroom. It was too painful to keep going up and down. A friend from church helped me by getting a bath stool and a pair of crutches to get around on. I have been very unsettled and my stomach is very bloated, the pressure starts to build and it affects my throat and head.

I cannot concentrate and I'm feeling anxiety and fear. I am panicking most of the time, feeling that I'm unable to breathe. I am trying to calm down, my throat is dry and I am feeling thirsty, but I'm afraid to drink some water as it might stop me from breathing. I won't even take a bath because I feel I might drown.

I got up this morning feeling low and did not want to pray. I felt condemned, I told myself that 'I love me, there is no condemnation and that God is love.' Dave has made me some breakfast as it's the weekend. After breakfast I went on the internet looking for anything on healing and restoration, also I needed to know how to pray.

I have desires in my heart. I want to know God more and about the life he has for me. I want to know his plans for me. I want to move on with my life. I want my wounds healed. I want the desire to seek God with all my heart and soul. I am thinking now about what I can do? Dave says "I love you Bal, I love you."

I wept and wept. Dave told me that I'm a wonderful mother; wife and a wonderful person, and then he said to me "Don't you forget it." Dave also talked to me about not being too hard on myself.

Prayers are peaceful; talking to God is having a relationship and also fun. I was having old thoughts telling me that I don't deserve God's blessings. I would say "You're right; I know I don't deserve it but that's what Gods mercy and grace is all about." I would say to myself 'keep going and look forward to the future.'

I felt so alone, I'm crying and crying "is anyone going to help me?" I felt as if I was going to die. How can I understand, how is all this happening? It's been months now and I'm waiting to see the surgeon as I've had a MRI and a CT scan. The results of the tests are here and the scans have shown that on the lower spine the bone has chipped and it's crushing the nerves that go to the left leg.

Nine months have passed before the Doctor at the hospital said that I will need a double operation on the spine to remove some of the disc and some bone. Otherwise if I tripped and fell again I could be paralysed from the waist down. I wanted peace of mind so I ask the doctor lots of questions about the treatment and medical help and care.

I have been house bound, unable to walk, do housework and unable to cook. A few times I had friends from church bring meals for the whole family and on a couple of occasions family members bought meals also.

I have put a rota together where the house work will be shared between the three children. I have asked Dave to buy me a stool so I can sit in the kitchen and cook the best I can. The time has come for me to go into hospital for the operation. I am nervous as the operation is going to take a few hours. Dave is with me for a while and then I had to go into another waiting room.

I have been waiting now for six hours on my own before they decided that they will operate on my spine even though it is late in the evening. After the operation I remember being in so much excruciating pain that I've been given morphine to ease it. I was going to be in hospital until I was able to sit up in bed. For the first couple of days I had to stay lying flat, then each day moving up until I could do my best to sit up so I could come home. The day has come and I am going home. I have thanked the nurses for looking after me; I gave them a box of chocolates and a thank you card.

Another start to my journey to recovery and I am back upstairs where most of my time was spent. My husband and my children have been a blessing to me, looking after me when I needed it most. I was not used to being bed ridden because I was always taking care of the family. I would do my best to look after my personal care; even though it was difficult.

It has been a few weeks now and I'm walking upstairs with crutches. When I needed a shower or bath I would always wait until someone was always at home. I had a bath stool that I used when having a shower, but the water would go all over the place soaking the floor, so I decided I would try and have a shower without it and stand in the bath. I was doing so well until I slipped, took a turn, banging my hip on the side of the bath and fell with a thud. Dave came running upstairs calling out to me "What has happened? I'm going to kick the door in" I said "I am OK, don't do that please." I was so embarrassed to say otherwise because I wanted to do things as before.

I have been able to come down stairs by walking backwards holding onto the banister rail then using the crutches to get around. It has been a struggle and most of the time I am bored so I've decided to be creative and started to knit. My mother-in- law Maureen has given me a pair of knitting needles so I got some wool.

After weeks and weeks I finally made a shoulder bag which I put some lining into it. Then I knitted a phone case for Sarah and Thomas before I got bored of it. I needed another hobby so I started number painting which I enjoyed and did many paintings. I would also enjoy doing word searches.

I would do the cooking by standing and would be supported by the work surface. That was enjoyable until one day I lost my balance and fell whilst I was holding a pot of water. It felt weird because it was like stopping a goal, I fell to the left with the pot of water, the pot landed in the sink, as I fell I missed hurting my head on the exposed pipes. I believe I was protected by angels.

I have a hospital appointment to see the progress of my spine as its healing well and I'll be having physiotherapy and exercises classes. The doctor had told me that if the dropped foot doesn't heal within three years then I would have to wear a foot brace.

I didn't like what I was hearing, 'no that can't be true, I will walk again' I cried. At home I am having negative thoughts; I cried a lot, I had so much anger and frustration that I hit my crutches on the table. Dave and I took a walk in the garden to help me calm down. I was thinking 'Would I be wearing shoes again? What about high heels and sandals?'

When I went grocery shopping with Dave I would go in one of the scooters Asda provided and I would ask Dave to put shopping in my basket. Some shoppers would look at me as if they were thinking "There is nothing wrong with her." I would get so paranoid that I wouldn't want to go out. I had to encourage myself so that I didn't give up. I asked Dave to help me walk out of the house and as I carefully walked a few steps down the driveway it felt such an achievement. Every day I made an effort to walk outside the house and I was now able to walk a few yards.

I was so excited that I knocked on the neighbour's door to say hello; I was happy that I had walked that distance. I had set backs I found it frustrating and hard to continue but it had to be done. Dave always encouraged me knowing that I was not a quitter. We would go for walks together, each time I would add a few extra steps.

I had applied for sick benefit as I'm not able to work, but when I had a medical I was refused any benefits. If that wasn't bad enough I couldn't get any other benefits because I didn't have enough national contributions; I was gutted. I tried and asked for help finding employment, but I felt I was put in the deep end; I felt unable to cope. I had lost all confidence not being able to walk properly as I had always been independent and always looked after the family. Dave said he would look after me and my children and support us, the bills were always paid and we always had food on the table.

I was given a debit card to spend money as I needed to but I struggled with it, I would ask Dave if he would just hand me some money instead. The next appointment I had was in the hospitals Orthotics department where I was measured for a foot support. A plastic foot brace has been made to support my foot and the only shoes I could wear with it were trainers. These trainers would hold the brace, which had a Velcro band fastened around my calf and my foot would sit on top of it. When I first wore the foot brace I was so pleased to be able to walk properly for the first time in ages.

It took me a while to adjust walking on the brace as it would hurt my foot and leave an imprint on my sole. I didn't like it on show so I would always wear boot cut jeans. It was so much hassle putting it on and off while I was in the house, wanting to rest and then walk. Each day that went by I would see the unfinished extension and also see the amount of work that still needed doing.

I was adamant that each day I would do some jobs little by little, this was because Dave had a full time job, Michael and Sarah were both working and Thomas had just graduated from university and was looking for employment. Thomas didn't want a fuss at his graduation so we had a small celebration.

We continued going to church on Sundays and I would read my little red bible. As I was reading this verse in Proverbs 1:9 *what you learn from them will crown you with grace and a chain of honour around your neck'*.

I thought to myself that this has never happened to me, but then I had a flash back that reminded me of the time that my Dad honoured me with a gold chain for the time I looked after him. He took me to the jewellery shop and bought me a gold necklace of my choice. Oh my! The tears that came flooding out, I had sold it when I sold all the other gold.

How was I ever going to get it back? I was so remorseful and I cried to Father God hoping that one day I would get it back.

At one of the church services a guy named Chris asked if he could pray for me. I knew who he was so I had said yes. As he began praying for healing he noticed that I was getting emotional and holding it in at the same time. He asked me if I was OK, I started to cry as I was in excruciating pain; he continued to pray.

I felt my twisted leg being straightened. I thanked God as only He knew me inside and out. I had received a healing and this continued to give me hope. I thanked Chris for praying and he said he felt it in his heart to do so.

My health was putting pressure on mine and Dave's relationship I was getting more and more anxious and so frustrated that I would wake up in the early hours of the morning and come downstairs to read the Word and pray.

When I went back to bed I started to talk with Dave about it. I was telling him about all the painful issues about our relationship and family. Then as I tried to go back to sleep; Dave held my hand.

I said to him "After all I have said you want to hold my hand?" The words he spoke were love, compassion, sympathy and understanding. I stayed quiet and those words came into my heart like a plaster that had been placed on a wound.

My Life Now

When Dave had time off work he would continue working on the house. He suggested that I could design the kitchen and have any style that I wanted. At first I didn't care about it, until I started to dream and visualise the kitchen as being a top of the range one. At the moment it was the old with the new extension; the walls were bare and showing the breeze blocks. As it was summer Dave plumbed the sink and wired the electric cooker to use in the garden. He did this so that we had somewhere to cook whilst the old kitchen was taken out.

This took many weeks to do because it had to be plastered and then we had to wait for the plaster to dry. We then painted the kitchen and Dave put down laminate flooring. When the kitchen guy came to measure up, I knew exactly where I wanted the draws to go and the style I had created. This included a pull out larder, which I had always wanted.

I was so pleased with the outcome and how it looked that I called it the 'top of the range' kitchen. Dave worked so hard doing the DIY and everything we did to the house we did it together. The young adults in the family would help with the painting and wallpaper stripping. Bringing the plans and our dreams together took us almost four years.

Every year when it came to my birthday, Dave would ask me want I wanted. Each time I would say that there was nothing that I needed as I have got everything that I could ever wish for. That didn't help Dave though. As the days were getting closer to my birthday, I thought of a gift. I mentioned to Dave that I would like to have the same gold necklace that my Dad had bought me. It had to be the same style and weight. So we went to the same jewellery shop and I asked if they had the same style as when my Dad bought me the chain. The lady said that it was not available anymore and suggested that I choose a modern chain, which I didn't want.

We carried on looking and went to another jewellery shop. I described the chain and the weight that I was looking for, the assistant then asked me to draw the pattern that I was after. She had shown me so many but I was not going to give up hoping. After looking some more she came back with another tray of chains and took one out.

When I saw her holding it up I knew straight away that was the one. I said to her "that's the one, that's it." I was so pleased that I told her that we would take it, I asked her to weigh the gold but it was slightly lighter than the one my Dad brought me. I thought 'no, it can't be.' It was when she asked me to try it on that I noticed the clasp wasn't good so I asked for it to be replaced with a lobster claw clasp; which was it more secure. After the adjustment was made and the clasp fitted, she weighed the chain again. She was so surprised that she asked me to come around to her side of the desk so she could show me the weight.

It was the exact weight of the one that my Dad bought me. I felt so blessed that I said "Thank you Jesus" and "Thank you Dave." The shop lady was so amazed that she said that it was God's work. She happened to be a Christian.

The same month as my birthday in May, Dave, Sarah and I went to a conference in Telford where a speaker named Andrew Wommack was preaching the word of God. The place was almost full and we got seats right at the back of the hall. After the sermon he called people forward to receive Jesus. Around two hundred and fifty people came forward. Also people were called forward to receive the baptism of tongues and said that everyone who came forward would receive a free book.

 Where I was sitting I spoke the words gently and asked God if I could have a book, I then laughed with Sarah. Later on Dave, Sarah and I went forward for prayers. While waiting in the queue for prayers I sat down on the front row and on the chair next to me was a box; I peered over and saw a book. I got up and asked an usher if I could have a book and she asked me if I had received Jesus today; I replied no. However, she went to the box to get me a book and looked inside. She was speechless, it was the only book left in the box. Praise God! I knew it was left for me. I was amazed that God heard my whisper.

The following day we went to the second session and purchased one of Andrew Wommack's books which I was hoping to get signed. After lunch I saw a long queue and I asked the lady in front what the queue was for? She said it was for the book signing. I joined the queue and after a couple of minutes had passed it was announced that the second half of the conference was due to start; the queue disappeared. I saw Andrew Wommack having his picture taken with a couple. I went up to him and asked him if he would sign my book, he said yes and he did. Again I praised God.

During our time at church Dave and I completed a Mission Training College (MTC) course. We went deep into the word of God and it felt like I was going back to school; where we had to do write essays. Each time I would be the first one to hand in the essay. After the eightieth month course had come to completion; we passed and received a graduation certificate.

At this time in my life I am a home maker, a blessed wife and a proud mum.

To The Reader

"I hope my testimony has encouraged you to never give up and to keep on going. I did not make it this far on my own but by the Grace of God through acceptance of Jesus Christ as my Lord and Saviour.

Accept Jesus Christ now, by asking Him to come into your heart, he will come and He will help you in ways unimaginable".

For God so loved the world, that He gave his only begotten Son, that whosoever believeth in Him should not perish, but have everlasting life. John 3:16

God Bless

Printed in Great Britain
by Amazon